doing business in thailand

doing business in thailand

The essential guide to commerce for foreigners

PETER NORTH & BEA TOEWS

mc **Marshall Cavendish**
Business

Published in 2014 by Marshall Cavendish Business
An imprint of Marshall Cavendish International
1 New Industrial Road, Singapore 536196

Other Marshall Cavendish Offices:
Marshall Cavendish Corporation. 99 White Plains Road, Tarrytown NY 10591-9001, USA • Marshall Cavendish International (Thailand) Co Ltd. 253 Asoke, 12th Flr, Sukhumvit 21 Road, Klongtoey Nua, Wattana, Bangkok 10110, Thailand • Marshall Cavendish (Malaysia) Sdn Bhd, Times Subang, Lot 46, Subang Hi-Tech Industrial Park, Batu Tiga, 40000 Shah Alam, Selangor Darul Ehsan, Malaysia.

Marshall Cavendish is a trademark of Times Publishing Limited

National Library Board, Singapore Cataloguing-in-Publication Data:

North, Peter, 1943–
Doing Business in Thailand : the essential guide to commerce for foreigners / Peter North & Bea Toews. – Singapore : Marshall Cavendish Business, 2014.
pages cm

ISBN : 978-981-4516-06-8 (paperback)

1. Small business – Foreign ownership – Guidebooks. 2. Small business – Thailand – Guidebooks. 3. Business enterprises – Foreign ownership – Guidebooks.
4. Business enterprises – Thailand – Guidebooks.
I. Toews, Bea. II. Title.
HD2341
338.0409595 – dc23   OCN 882152270

Cover design by Bernard Go Kwang Meng

Printed in Singapore by Times Printers Pte Ltd

Contents

Introduction

This book is intended as an information guide for foreigners considering working or doing business in Thailand. The book aims to help:

- Anyone intending to establish a business in Thailand
- Those already doing business in Thailand who seek further guidance through the maze of permissions and licences of the Thai government bureaucracy
- Expats intending to work in Thailand
- Importers or exporters of goods in and out of Thailand
- Passive investors in Thailand
- Tourists to Thailand intending to find part-time jobs

Southeast Asia is the world's fastest-growing region economically. The prospective investor has a choice of developing economies in which to invest. While this book is about Thailand, we have tried to avoid bias in considering Thailand's attractions and drawbacks to a potential investor. Our aim is to provide objective data on which interested parties can base their decisions.

Since no book of this size can include the vast volume of data now available in literature and on the internet, let alone update information as it changes, English-language internet references relevant to topics discussed are included in the text. From this wide range of sources, readers of the book can keep themselves updated on markets, regulations, costings and other data as required. A complete list of referenced websites is included at the back of the book.

Businesses that foreigners might wish to establish in Thailand range from branches of multi-national corporations like auto companies, to small enterprises such as restaurants, bars, and strip shopping retail outlets. As well as attractions, foreigners face pitfalls in establishing business in Thailand, particularly in the small-business area, where the barriers are considerable and the casualty rate is high. Anecdotal accounts of failed and successful foreign-owned small businesses in Thailand have been published in a number of books, some of which are included in the bibliography attached. By contrast the intention of this book is to provide facts and figures on business operations in Thailand, rather than a series of case studies.

We start the book by considering the likely effect on business of the unstable Thai political situation which was much in the news at the beginning of 2014. From there we move to markets for specific major industry segments, manufacturing, finance and services. We then provide details of financial incentives available to investors, costing data, capital requirements, banking procedures, taxation laws, legal issues, staffing and manpower, infrastructure and environment.

In the book we refer to a number of Acts of Parliament relating to business in Thailand. These acts have been translated into English and can be readily downloaded. Extracts from the Thai lawbook pertinent to particular topics are included in the text.

On the managerial level, once a business has been established, an important topic is how Thais and expats are likely to interact in a business setting. Stemming from sources steeped in the country's history, culture in Thailand is intricate and complex. Protocol at all levels of society is perhaps more important in Thailand than most other countries. That said, Thais are tolerant of their visitors' sometimes bizarre behaviour. They do not expect foreigners to have mastered every nuance of the "Thai way" of doing things. On the other hand, to avoid jeopardising your relationships by perpetrating some unintended insult, it's worth taking pains to acquire a working knowledge of Thai culture.

In addition to advice about business activities, the book gives an account of the economic climate and political events that have shaped the cultural environment of Thailand. Thais prefer to avoid conflict in their dealings with other people. Preserving community harmony is a principal reason for their complex rules of behaviour when Thais interact with foreigners and one another in their respective roles as customers, staff, employers, suppliers, advisors and government.

That citizens of the "Land of Smiles" are some of the friendliest people on Earth is a widely held belief that we endorse. Thailand is a great place to live. While the Thai way of doing business can be challenging for foreigners, it can also be fun and rewarding.

Thailand at a Glance

Country

Area	513,120 sq km – about the same as Spain
Land boundaries	4,864 km
Coastline	3,219 km
Climate	Mostly tropical, with southwest monsoon from May to October, and mostly dry for the balance of the year, except in the south
Capital	Bangkok
Population	67 million
Literacy	93.5%

Economy

GDP (PPP method)	US$673 billion
GDP (Exchange rate)	US$400 billion
GDP per capita	US$9,900 (PPP method)
GDP by sector	Agriculture 12.2%, Industry 43.6%, Services 44.2%
Growth rate	2.9% (2013 estimate); 6.5% (2012)
Government debt	45.9% of GDP
Inflation rate	2.2%
Exports	US$225 billion
Imports	US$219 billion
Major exports	Electronics, computer parts, automobiles and parts, electrical appliances, machinery and equipment, textiles and footwear, fishery products, rice, rubber
Major imports	Capital goods, intermediate goods and raw materials, consumer goods, fuels (oil, gas and coal)
Major export destinations (2012)	China 11.7%, Japan 10.2%, United States 9.9%, Hong Kong 5.7%, Malaysia 5.4%, Indonesia 4.9%, Singapore 4.7%, Australia 4.3%
Major import sources (2012)	Japan 20%, China 14.9%, UAE 6.3%, Malaysia 5.3%, United States 5.3%

Source: CIA Factbook – 2013 estimates
(www.cia.gov/library/publications/the-world-factbook/geos/th.html)

Chapter 1

Investment Climate in Thailand

Politics and business

Towards the end of 2013 and into the beginning of 2014, the world media carried images of political demonstrations in Bangkok. Key intersections in the capital were blocked. Chairs were placed on major city roads to accommodate protesters who had gathered to view anti-government political speeches on large TV screens set up at strategic points. Public transport systems operated reduced services.

Not wishing to inflame the situation, the government adopted a hands-off approach, hoping disturbances would die down of their own accord.

They didn't.

Instead violent clashes between the opposing political sides – the Red Shirts and the Yellow Shirts – brought a rising death toll in the early months of 2014. After it became apparent that squabbling politicians were unlikely to resolve the imbroglio themselves, the army stepped in to take over. Martial law was declared on 20 May 2014. At time of writing, this is the status.

Foreigners might wonder what could so stir the passions of people who otherwise seem so laidback to take to the streets en masse. What might motivate gangs of otherwise peace-loving citizens to march through the city brandishing slogans and blowing whistles? And why would the government allow the streets of the capital to be blockaded for months on end? And maybe of greatest importance to prospective foreign investors, how might the prolonged civil unrest affect the investment climate?

More sanguine observers pointed out that demonstrations in Bangkok are not out of the ordinary. In the last 25 years, Thailand has experienced four military coups and had 20 prime ministers, five of whom were generals appointed by the army.

At the root of the conflict is a deep-seated rivalry between the "Red Shirts" and the "Yellow Shirts", with whichever group not currently holding political power mounting protests against the other.

This political squabble originated in 2001, when the Red Shirts' political party under the then prime minister, Thaksin Shinawatra, won power for the first time, was re-elected in 2005, and was later ousted in a military coup.

During the last days of the Thaksin government, the Yellow Shirt protesters took over Bangkok Airport. After the 2006 coup, Red Shirt protesters took to the streets in a series of demonstrations which culminated in the burning down of Bangkok's World Trade Centre in 2010. While images of political action in the streets of Bangkok in 2013 and 2014 were beamed to a startled world, to some Thais street demonstrations in Bangkok seemed almost situation normal – even tame by comparison with the recent past.

There are no great ideological differences between Thailand's two sides of politics. Both sides are pro-business, since most Thai politicians are themselves business people. What they are arguing about is not any fundamental policy difference, rather their entitlement to power.

As a result, to the surprise of some commentators, mainstream business has pretty much ignored the years of chronic mayhem in the country's leadership. With business-friendly policies on both sides of politics, investment in the country has continued through many coups and changes of government. Against a chaotic political background spanning decades, the country has gone about its business, built a modern infrastructure, established a dynamic industry base, posted impressive economic growth figures, run a positive balance on external trade and greatly alleviated poverty.

In 2011 the World Bank formally recognised Thailand's progress on social and economic issues. The country had sustained a long period of strong growth, achieved manageable public debt, a generally positive balance of trade, low inflation, very low unemployment, impressive poverty reduction, and positive trade and current account balances (see www.worldbank.org/en/country/thailand/overview). Accordingly the Bank upgraded Thailand from a lower-middle-income economy to an upper-middle-income economy – the same rating as for China and Malaysia.

Investment policies – some historical background

By the end of the 19th century, all of Thailand's bordering countries were administered by foreign powers – Burma and Malaysia (including present-day Singapore) by Britain, and Laos, Cambodia and Vietnam by France. Thais are proud that their country (then known as Siam) is the only Southeast Asian nation never colonised by a European power, either politically or economically.

Thailand's intention to remain a self-sufficient economic power free of foreign control runs through history to the present day. Regulations regarding inward investment by foreigners have been written accordingly.

Until the 1960s, Thailand was primarily an agricultural economy trading commodities such as rice, rubber, maize, sugar cane and seafood. For the most part, the countryside is still a patchwork of smallholdings of rice-growers rather than broad-acre farms. Much of the rural population, particularly women, still plant and harvest and thresh their rice crops by hand as they did a thousand years ago. In many locations oxen still plough the fields. Barefoot, saffron-clad monks mingle with the population. The smallest village has a temple that historically provided the community its inspiration, culture, administration and education.

Should you be unfamiliar with Thailand and its people, we suggest you might get a feel for the country by reading its history.

Thailand: A Short History by David K. Wyatt is regarded by many as the standard English-language text on this subject.

By the mid-1960s, major changes to the country's economy were afoot. With an influx of American troops waging the Vietnam War, the country's fledgling tourism industry began to develop. At about this time, the government launched its industrial investment programme. At first Thailand concentrated on producing local equivalents of imported goods. The emphasis changed in the early 1980s, when the country switched its focus from import substitution to exporting.

The objective was, and still is, to follow the examples of the "Asian Tigers" – Japan, South Korea, Singapore and Taiwan – to obtain the benefits of industrialisation without selling out the country. Maintaining ownership of industry in Thai hands while acquiring technology from the First World remains a bedrock principle in Thai industrial policy. This thinking has important implications for potential foreign investors, in particular (with some exceptions) that a foreign business establishing in Thailand requires Thai partners.

If the government thinks Thais have traditional rights to the industry, or thinks Thais can do the job without foreign input, rules restrict foreign ownership (usually to a maximum of 49%) and directorships (a majority of Thais is required). Various other rules apply, such as minimum capital requirements and the minimum number of Thais the business must employ.

Foreign Business Act

The principal law governing the rights, obligations and entitlements of foreign businesses operating in Thailand is the Foreign Business Act (FBA) of 1999 (refer to www.thailawforum.com/database1/foreign.html). What Thailand wants from foreign business is described in Section 5 of the FBA:

In permitting foreigners to operate businesses under this act, the advantages and disadvantages to the nation's safety and security, economic and social development, public order or good morals, art, culture and tradition of the country, natural resource conservation, energy and environment, consumer protection, size of the enterprises, employment, technology transfer, and research and development are all taken into account.

In general terms, this policy favours high-tech industries with export potential, import-replacing industries, industries with minimal environmental impact and industries like renewable energy that improve the country's balance of trade and reduce its dependence on imported fossil fuels, in particular oil. Businesses conducting activities perceived as bringing fewer benefits to the country get less favoured treatment.

Lists of restricted business activity are included as an attachment to the FBA. Restricted businesses are divided into three categories:

- **List 1** – Entirely prohibited to aliens (foreigners) under all circumstances, this category includes traditional agriculture pursuits such as rice-growing, fishing and animal husbandry; newspapers, radio, TV; owning land; and making certain religious and culturally significant items, e.g. Buddha statutes.

- **List 2** – This category is prohibited to aliens unless approval is granted by the Board of Investment, and includes industries relating to military activities, arts and culture and exploiting natural resources.

- **List 3** – Businesses under this category are open to aliens (foreigners), but under a range of restrictions which depend on factors such as the nature of the business, its location, the presence or absence of Thai partners, and the nationality of the foreign applicant. List 3 includes a wide range of service industries such as advisory services and retailing.

List 1 and 2 are off-limits to foreigners. A foreigner desiring to do a business specified in List 3 must submit an application to the Department of Commercial Registration of the Ministry of Commerce (see Section 29 of the FBA). A permit issued by the department is normally valid for a fixed period, but sometimes without limit, and is subject to conditions.

These three lists are not all-inclusive. Really the only way to determine a status for your proposed business is to apply for a licence, the issuance of which depends not only on what you intend to do, but on how you phrase your intentions on your application.

Notably absent from these lists of restricted businesses is manufacturing, which is the activity for which a 100% foreign-owned business is most likely to be granted a licence.

Amendments and exceptions to the FBA

Various treaties may modify these foreign ownership rules. A special case is the Treaty of Amity and Economic Relations signed in 1966 and ratified in 1968 between the US and Thailand. The Amity Treaty allows US citizens, or companies incorporated in the US, to engage in business in Thailand on the same basis as Thais. In return, Thais are extended reciprocal rights in the US.

As a result, a US corporation may set up a wholly owned subsidiary company or branch office in Thailand with restrictions only in the fields of communications, transport, banking, exploiting land or natural resources, and agriculture. To register under the Treaty, a US company needs to file an application with the Department of Commercial Registration, Ministry of Commerce.

Theoretically the Amity Treaty expired in 2005. However, the Thai government agreed to extend the treaty conditions for a further period while Free Trade Agreement negotiations were conducted between the two countries. At time of writing, the Amity Treaty, which is seen in Thailand as favouring the US, is still in force.

Somewhat less liberal ownership concessions have also been extended to Australia under TAFTA (Thailand Australia Free Trade Agreement) of 2005.

As well as its specific treaty obligations to the US and Australia, Thailand will also be subject to future regulations with the ASEAN Economic Community (AEC), due to come into force in 2015. Under new arrangements, and with certain reservations, ASEAN investors will have the right to own up to 70% of Thai companies, whatever their products or services. Similar arrangements may later come into force under trade agreements Thailand has with wider trading groups such as APEC. Those interested in obtaining further details on this subject can refer to the webpage on Foreign Business Restrictions at www.bia.co.th/005.html.

Ease of doing business in Thailand

In its publication *Doing Business 2014*, the World Bank presents an index assessing how easy it is for foreigners to start and operate a small to medium sized enterprise (SME) in 189 of the world's countries. The index considers such factors as ownership of land and other assets, issuance of construction permits, availability and connection to utilities, obtaining finance, taxation, rules relating to imports and exports, entering and enforcing contracts, bankruptcy laws and legislative protection afforded to investors.

According to the index, in 2013 Singapore, Hong Kong, China, New Zealand and the USA were the five easiest countries in which to do business. ASEAN countries were ranked as follows: Malaysia (6), Thailand (18), Brunei (59), Vietnam (99), Philippines (108), Indonesia (120), Laos (159), Myanmar (182) and Cambodia (187). For the full listing, refer to www.doingbusiness.org.

The three most favourable factors in Thailand's index were getting electricity (12), protecting investors (12) and dealing with construction permits (14). Its least favourable categories were paying taxes (70), obtaining credit (73) and starting the business (90).

The first year for which the World Bank published its Ease of Doing Business Index was 2005. Since then, Thailand's rating has stayed the same for some factors and improved for others, meaning that over the period 2005–2013, Thailand has become an easier place than it once was for foreigners to do business in.

It will probably become easier still once the ASEAN Economic Community rules are in place.

Corruption

Thailand's institutions, particularly police and customs, have often been criticised for corruption. Some commentators see corruption

in Thailand as having its roots in the earlier days of absolute mon-
archies, when unpaid government officials made their money by
taking a percentage of the taxes they collected before turning the
balance over to the royal treasury.

Today, government officials are paid, but not much, and old
habits die hard. Cash applied at opportune moments when dealing
with the Thai bureaucracy can yield favourable results. That much
of the wider Thai community regards an unofficial payment to a
government officer as a service charge or a goodwill gift (*sin nam
chai*) rather than a bribe perpetuates the system.

Transparency International (TI) reports each year on perceived
corruption around the world. The report assesses levels of corruption within various nations based on reports of ratings agencies, risk management agencies, international accounting firms,
and other stakeholders who have dealings with countries in the
survey. The corruption level for each country, termed the Corruption Perception Index (CPI), is assessed as a point score between
zero (most corrupt) and 100 (least corrupt).

In 2013, TI assessed corruption levels in 177 countries. New Zealand and Denmark tied as the world's least corrupt countries, with
North Korea and Afghanistan the most corrupt. Thailand came in
number 102 on this survey, with a score of 35.

According to TI, any country that scores less than 50 on this
survey *has a serious corruption problem*. To put this into perspec-
tive, 70% of the countries surveyed scored less than 50, including
most of Thailand's ASEAN trading partners (the exceptions were
Singapore (86) and Malaysia (50)). On this basis, if Transparency
International is to be believed, *most of the world has serious corruption problems*.

TI's definition of corruption – "the misuse of public power for
private benefit" – seems to fit the situation in Thailand. A country
which turns over politicians for corruption offences as often as
Thailand does would seem to have a chronic corruption problem
that isn't being seriously addressed. On the other hand, in the opinion of some long-term residents of Asia, corrupt practices that are
now being exposed in the media are not really new. What is new is

that they are being exposed. Practices quietly accepted in the past now incur public criticism, suggesting that corruption is increasing when it may actually be declining. Viewed optimistically, this could indicate that Asian societies are less willing to tolerate practices that, just a few years ago, were accepted as part of the cultural fabric. In the past few decades, Indonesia has experienced a more extreme version of the process.

One final word on corruption: though it may exist in government, the army and the public service, in our experience Thais in small businesses like retail and restaurants are honest to a fault. Many times we have been chased down the street and urged to repossess small change that we left as a tip. Refunds for items bought at marked prices, but which were marked down, have been pressed into our hands. Items like cameras and passports that we carelessly left in shops were stored away and returned to us on our next visit – always with a smile and best wishes from the retailer, and with the offered reward declined.

Small Business versus Big Business

Ownership rules in Thailand favour industries that the country perceives as being in its interests. While the policy doesn't specifically discriminate against small business, large manufacturing businesses will be treated more favourably by the Thai government than a foreigner who wants to open up a bar in Pattaya. As mentioned in the introduction, case studies of failed and successful small foreign operated businesses in Thailand are beyond the scope of this book, but is the subject of some of the books listed in the attached bibliography. The best prospects for small business in Thailand are probably in high-tech areas such as consultancy, software development and renewable energy projects. Business opportunities for specific industry sectors for both small and large businesses are considered in more detail later in the book.

Chapter 2

Where You Can Get Help

Thai Board of Investment (BOI)
The principal body charged with encouraging investment in Thailand is the Board of Investment (BOI), a department of the Ministry of Industry. The BOI was established through the Investment Promotion Act of 1977. Its charter is to promote development of Thai strategic industries. To this end, the BOI can be of major assistance to both local and foreign SMEs considering setting up operations in Thailand. BOI benefits come in three forms: advice, financial incentives and smoothing the path through Thai bureaucracy.

Advice
The BOI will assist with information regarding setting up a business in Thailand. Free of charge, it will advise on corporate formation, corporate structures, taxation, licensing requirements, tax rates, labour costs and the cost of doing business in Thailand.

Incentives
Acceptance of a project by the BOI comes with significant financial tax and other benefits, including:

- Reduction of or exemption from corporate income tax
- Reduction of or exemption from tariffs on imports
- Reduction of personal income tax

- Accelerated depreciation
- Favourable land deals, including permission to own land
- Permission to remit money offshore

Allowances and benefits will vary depending on the industry and the geographical zone in which the project is located. For a complete explanation of obligations and rewards under BOI investment promotion schemes, you can download the Guide to the Board of Investment 2013 from the BOI website (www.boi.go.th). The Thai embassy and consulate in your home country can also help you get current BOI information.

Assistance
As an additional convenience to private businesses embarking on investment projects in Thailand, in October 2010 the Department of Business Development opened its One Start One Stop (OSOS) investment centre.

OSOS offers assistance for the following activities:

- Corporate registration
- Processing paperwork to obtain investment privileges
- Obtaining foreign (to Thailand) business licences
- Preparing environmental impact statements
- Obtaining permissions for using land for industrial purposes
- Assisting in utility connections
- Registering for social security
- Registering for the Workers' Compensation Fund
- Assisting in obtaining visas and work permits
- Directing investors to appropriate agencies for matters that lie outside the charter of OSOS

Further details of OSOS assistance can be found on the BOI website. The physical location of OSOS is in the CBD of Bangkok, on the 18th floor of Chamchuri Square Building, 319 Phayathai Road, Pathumwan, Bangkok 10330. E-mail queries can be addressed to osos@boi.go.th; more information is available at osos.boi.go.th.

BOI's decentralisation policy

BOI's principal objective at its formation during the 1970s was to promote the industrialisation of the country. A shift in emphasis in the 1990s added decentralisation as an additional policy goal, with the object of encouraging development outside the Bangkok metropolitan area.

While making goods for export is still the number one item on the government's industry agenda, a secondary objective is to develop regional industry. Your application for BOI privileges is more likely to succeed if your project is located outside the national capital.

To further define the decentralisation objective, the Thai government has adopted several methods of dividing the country into economic zones. The industrialisation policy assigns the country's 76 provinces to one of three Zones, roughly based on their distance from Bangkok:

- **Zone 1** – Bangkok, Nakhon Pathom, Nonthaburi, Pathum Thani, Samut Prakan, and Samut Sakhon
- **Zone 2** – Ang Thong, Ayutthaya, Chachoengsao, Chon Buri, Kanchanaburi, Nakorn Nayok, Ratchaburi, Samut Songkhram, Saraburi, Supanburi, Phuket and Rayong.
- **Zone 3** – The remaining provinces. These are the regions the government is most eager to industrialise, in particular areas bordering neighbouring countries like Cambodia and Myanmar.

Industrial Estate Authority of Thailand (IEAT)

Working with the BOI is an organization called the Industrial Estate Authority of Thailand (IEAT). The mission of IEAT is develop and manage large industrial estates in Thailand. In the spirit of Silicon Valley in the US or Bangalore in India, the intent is to concentrate particular industries into specialist industrial parks so that neighbouring companies engaged in similar activities may enjoy economies of scale. For example, an industrial park in the Ayutthaya area accommodates companies in the computer component industry and another industrial park in the same general area is home to auto companies and associated component manufacturers.

IEAT manages operations at its estates with authority to allocate sites, issue licences for investors, and organise the provision of utilities. IEAT also has authority to impose construction standards, check building quality and deal with issues such as emissions of gases and liquids to the environment. By 2013 there were 47 industrial parks in Thailand, with the greatest concentration of heavy industry parks in the eastern coastal provinces of Rayong (11 parks) and Chonburi (7). Over the years a nucleus of large foreign high-tech companies have established operations in BOI's technology parks, enabling a network of smaller Thai-owned component supply businesses to establish themselves in the same parks.

For information on which type of industry is located in which park, refer to the guide prepared by the IEAT available at www.thaiembassy.org/kotabharu/contents/files/business-20120625-150818-476125.pdf, or check out the webpage on industrial estates at www.thaiwebsites.com/industrialestates.asp. For further information on availability of sites in industrial parks and benefits to particular locations, visit the IEAT homepage at www.ieat.go.th (the website is in Thai, but can be translated into the language of your choice with Google Translate for a general idea of the content).

Export Processing Zones

To accommodate heavy industry such as chemical plants and hydrocarbon processing facilities, Free Trade Zones, or Export Processing Zones (EPZ), exist in coastal areas near deep-water ports. Thailand has 10 EPZs at coastal locations across the country. Firms located in EPZs are exempt from import duties and taxes on factory construction materials, machinery and equipment, and export manufacturing inputs.

EPZs are managed by IEAT in a similar manner to industrial estates. Similar benefits and concessions apply. In addition, within EPZs, the Customs Department allows larger firms engaged exclusively in manufacturing for export to set up bonded warehouses and to import (duty-free) inputs for their export production. Producers who receive approval to establish bonded warehouses must pay an annual fee and submit guarantees for duties which would otherwise be payable. Further details can be obtained from the Thai Customs Department's website; the relevant information on EPZs is found at www2.customGs.go.th/Customs-Eng/EPZ/EPZ.

Industries favoured for BOI assistance

Applications for BOI assistance are more likely to be successful for some industry groups than others. In this regard, the BOI continually maintains and upgrades its list of economic activities considered to be in the national interest. Obligations on the investor are detailed in a number of Acts of Parliament, English translations of which can be downloaded from the internet by Googling the name of the act.

The Act of Parliament under which the BOI operates is the Investment Promotion Act B.E. 2520 (2002). Section 18 defines BOI's project evaluation criteria in the following words:

Consideration will be given to:
(1) The existing number of producers and production capacity in the kingdom and the size of production capacity to be created under promotion compared with demand estimates;
(2) The prospect for which such activity will expand the market for the products or commodities produced or assembled in the kingdom and will encourage the production or assembly in the kingdom;
(3) The quantity and proportion of the resources available in the kingdom including the capital, raw or essential materials and labour or other services utilised;
(4) The amount of foreign currency which may be saved or earned for the kingdom;
(5) The suitability of the production or assembly processes;
(6) Other requirements which the Board deems necessary and appropriate.

And that's not all. In addition to these criteria, the Guide to the Board of Investment 2013 states:

> Priority is given to agricultural activities and agricultural products, projects related to technological and human resource development, public utilities, infrastructure and basic services, environmental protection and conservation and targeted industries.

Obligations
Help from the BOI doesn't come without strings attached. Section 20 of the Investment Promotion Act reads:

> In the case where the Board deems it appropriate to grant promotion to any applicant, the Board may stipulate conditions in the promotion certificate for the compliance by the promoted person in one or more areas as follows:
> (1) Amount and source of capital;
> (2) Nationality and number of shareholders;
> (3) Size of activity including the types of products, commodities or services and the production or assembly processes, and capacity thereof;
> (4) Amount of local raw materials to be used;
> (5) Nationality and number of workers, technicians and experts;
> (6) Training and employment of manpower;
> (7) Prevention and control of damaging elements to the quality of the environment;
> (8) Period of time to commence the implementation of the promoted project;
> (9) Period of time to place orders for the purchase of machinery;
> (10) Period of time to import machinery into the kingdom;
> (11) Period of time re-export the imported machinery after the termination of their use;
> (12) Extension of time limits under (8), (9), or (11);

(13) Date of commencement of operation;

(14) Report on implementation of the project and operation;

(15) Report on the performance of the training provided by the foreign technicians and experts to the Thai personnel;

(16) Requirements that the products or commodities produced, assembled or exported conform to the standards prescribed either by the Board or other government agencies;

(17) Distribution of products or commodities produced or assembled, or services rendered;

(18) Export of products or commodities produced or assembled;

(19) Requirements that the cash, bank guarantee, the Thai government securities or other securities deemed appropriate by the Board, be deposited with the Office for the purpose of guaranteeing the compliance with the conditions stipulated by the Board;

(20) Other matters relating to the provision of facilities to the competent official, granting, exercising or controlling of the rights and benefits under this Act.

In addition the BOI imposes obligations such as an undertaking that the successful applicant qualify to Quality Standard ISO 9000 or equivalent.

Generally the BOI enjoys a good reputation with the foreign business community in Thailand. The BOI is considered to be transparent, helpful and for the most part empowered to accomplish its charter of assisting key industries establish and develop. The main reported downside for BOI clients is the BOI's requirement to submit copious feedback in the form of progress reports.

Applying for BOI assistance

Applicants for BOI assistance can download application forms from the BOI website and submit the application under their own steam (www.boi.go.th/index.php?page=form). But the BOI's website advises:

Sending applications to the Thailand BOI is best done through a Thai law firm as it's a very complex procedure. Contact us today to consult with any of our Thai lawyers or any number of our foreign lawyers on staff who will provide you with all the information you need.

To assist with applications, BOI recommends one of the legal firms listed on its webpage. As an alternative, prospective investors can obtain assistance at one of the fairs BOI runs from time to time. A timetable of BOI fairs can be downloaded from the BOI website.

If the business requires a Thai partner, the application must be submitted in the name of the joint venture, meaning that a company with Thai shareholders and directors must be formed as a first step. If no joint venture is required, the options are to apply in the name of the foreign firm, or to set up a Thai branch of the foreign firm before submitting the application. In most cases, the BOI will decide within 60 days whether or not a project is eligible for investment privileges.

To protect the interests of the successful applicants, and to maximise their chances of success, the BOI will generally only sponsor one applicant for any particular project at any particular time. Prospective investors should therefore note that foreign firms in similar industries may compete to win a BOI incentive package for their projects. That aside, BOI records confirm that assistance has been granted for about 80% of the applications submitted.

Within 15 days of approving a project, the BOI will issue the applicant a Notification of Approval. Within six months of receiving the Notification of Approval, the successful applicant must submit the following documents to the BOI:

- Memorandum of Association
- Certificate of Business Registration
- Certificate stating registered capital, list of authorised directors, and address of its head office

- List of shareholders
- A document evidencing remittance of foreign currency or a certificate of investment from overseas issued by the Bank of Thailand for foreign investors.
- Joint Venture Contract
- Completed application form to obtain the BOI's Promotion Certificate

At that point the BOI will issue the investor the Promotion Certificate, enabling the project to go ahead. The investor must start construction within six months of receiving the Promotion Certificate. Conditions of award stipulate that any machinery and equipment required for the project and exempted from import duties must be delivered within 24 months of the acceptance date and that construction of the facility must be completed within 30 months of the acceptance date. These safeguards might seem onerous to some. However, exclusion of other applicants from the same project does put some onus on the BOI to ensure that approved applicants are not dilatory about implementing their plans.

The following tables give various breakdowns of the projects sponsored by BOI in 2013 – by industry, zone, value and nationality of applicant:

Industry	%
Services & Infrastructure	38.1
Electronic & Electrical	20.0
Agriculture	16.2
Metal Manufacture	12.7
Chemical & Plastic	7.7
Light Industrial	3.5
Minerals	1.8

Zone	%
Zone 1	29.5
Zone 2	37.9
Zone 3	32.6

Value	%
Less than 20 million baht	26.3
20–200 million baht	42.5
200–500 million baht	13.1
500–1,000 million baht	10.3
Over 1,000 million baht	7.8

Nationality	%
Japan	26.2
Europe	7.8
Singapore	4.9
USA	3.4
Taiwan	2.6
Hong Kong	2.0
Others	53.1

The above statistics are drawn from the BOI website's Resource Centre. For a more specific list of industries supported by BOI, see Section 1.5 of Deloitte's *Taxation and Investment in Thailand 2013* (www2.deloitte.com/content/dam/Deloitte/global/Documents/Tax/dttl-tax-thailandguide-2013.pdf).

Financial modelling

Whether you register with BOI or not, prospective foreign investors into Thailand who require costing data to build financial models of their projects can access a comprehensive set of statistics from the BOI website. BOI's *Costs of Doing Business in Thailand 2014* is a 102-page English-language manual of the most comprehensive cost information for Thailand and is updated each year. It covers labour costs and entitlements by category, likely rents for different areas across the country, tax rates, utility costs, transport charges, costs for all forms of communication, costs of rental accommodation, and much more. In addition to costs of labour, entrepreneurs working in the business should add a minimum obligatory monthly salary paid to themselves of

25,000–60,000 baht (depending on nationality) as prescribed by legislation and on which income tax must be paid whether or not salaries are actually paid. (For further information, see www. thailandlawonline.com/thai-company-and-foreign-business-law/ work-permit-for-foreigners-in-thailand.)

Market research

The BOI may provide an idea of sizes of some markets. The Bureau of Statistics (web.nso.go.th) also publishes information for a wide range of products for the Thai market. Like other countries, Thailand has hundreds of marketing consultants specialising in various marketing sectors and ready to provide information for a fee.

If you have selected a prospective Thai partner already active in your industry, they will probably have made an assessment of the market for your product or service. However, Thais have a reputation for erring on the side of optimism. As a result, your Thai partner may have unrealistic expectations for your intended project. As the potential joint venturer supplying capital for the project, you would be wise to run some independent checks on your partner's market assessment.

Chapter 3

Specific Markets

While the Board of Investment caters for large-sized businesses up to assembly plants for major auto companies, there is no bottom limit to the size of business eligible for BOI support. However, greatly outnumbering BOI-sponsored businesses are thousands of part-foreign-owned smaller businesses operating in all sectors of the Thai economy. This chapter considers investment opportunities both large and small, whether supported by the BOI, or not.

Manufacturing

Thailand's industrial sector had its origins in adding value to agricultural products. From the post-war years up to the late 1950s, the major processing facilities included rice mills, sawmills, sugar mills, ice factories, footwear and textiles. Cottage industries included jewellery, fabric weaving, basketry, food processing and pottery to supply local needs. These traditional industries grew up in a free enterprise market. At that time, other than infrastructure projects, the government spent little investing in Thai industry.

In the 1980s, the government implemented the Investment Promotion Act (IPA). The purpose of the act was to foster import-replacement industries by instituting tariff protection and tax holidays for local companies making equivalents to imported goods. As an additional encouragement to local production, the IPA imposed high duties on imported raw materials and machinery. The focus of manufacture then shifted to exports. Industries producing electrical goods, transportation equipment, chemicals, paper products, office and scientific equipment became predominant.

This policy to foster export industries has continued to the present day.

Computer equipment and software

In the 1980s the BOI foresaw that computers and derivative products were at the beginning of a long period of expansion – one that has yet to end. The BOI promoted its industrial estates as locations for foreign companies to manufacture electronic components.

In 1991 the government formed a new entity, the National Science and Technology Development Agency (NSTDA), with the aim of advancing Thailand up the value chain from a component supplier to a manufacturer of stand-alone electronic products.

The electronics industry that resulted from this thinking has been one of Thailand's success stories. The best part of 30 years later, the industry accounts for over 30% of Thailand's exports and employs about 400,000 workers. Electronics is now the largest industry group in Thailand's manufacturing sector.

The major electronic products made in Thailand are hard disk drives (HDD), which account for about 21% of exports from the electronic sector. Thailand is now the world's second major producer of HDDs, after Singapore. During 2011, extensive floods in central Thailand closed down factories in both the electronics and the auto industry. Such was the importance of Thailand's production of HDDs that until the industry recovered from the flood, the world suffered a shortage of HDDs that persisted well into 2012.

Other major electronic products designed and manufactured in Thailand and widely exported are computer keyboards. The balance of exports from the sector are integrated circuits (ICs) and other hardware components.

On the software side, in 1997 NSTDA set up Software Park Thailand (SPT) to promote start-up firms along the Silicon Valley model. Since then, four other software parks across the country have been created. The largest of these, Thailand Science Park (TSP), established in 2002 and located about an hour north of Bangkok, hosts over 50 private companies, as well as the NSTDA headquarters and four government research bodies – the National Centre for Genetic Engineering and Biotechnology (BIOTEC), the National Metal and Material Technology Centre (MET), the National Electronics and Computer Technology Centre (NECTEC) and the National Nanotechnology Centre (NANOTEC).

Attractive incentives are available for firms wishing to create software, set up manufacturing facilities or enter into technology transfer arrangements with existing Thai companies. Further details can be obtained from NSTDA (www.nstda.or.th).

Motor vehicles and parts

Manufacture of automobiles and motorcycles is the second largest manufacturing industry in Thailand by value after computer components. Thailand's auto industry is the seventh largest in the world, with annual production of around 2.45 million vehicles.

The auto industry is concentrated in an area north of Bangkok near the ancient Siamese capital of Ayutthaya. Sixteen car companies have auto plants in Thailand, including all the world's largest manufacturers. These companies support a total of 2,400 component suppliers in the same geographical area. Foreign manufacturers involved in labour-intensive auto parts production take advantage of BOI investment incentive schemes that favour exporting industries (www.boi.go.th/index.php?page=opp_automotive).

Attractions to component suppliers considering setting up operations in Thailand are the presence of the major auto manufacturers, developed infrastructure, ready availability of trained low-cost labour, and a plentiful supply of raw materials, in particular rubber.

Like the computer industry, the auto industry is situated in the catchment area of the Chao Phraya River and its tributaries, and was badly affected by the 2011 floods. Disrupted operations of export businesses prompted the government to embark on an extensive flood-mitigation programme for fear the car companies might carry out their threats to leave Thailand and set up somewhere else if nothing was done to alleviate the worst effects of flooding. In response to this programme, the auto industry has continued to invest in this area, in 2012 committing about US$1 billion to expanding plants and facilities.

Energy

Hydrocarbon deposits in the Gulf of Thailand produce a small amount of oil and a larger amount of gas. In 2011, 39% of Thailand's energy consumption was from oil (80% imported), and 31% from natural gas (20% imported). The most significant alternative energy resource to hydrocarbons is biomass from by-products of the country's agricultural industries. Biomass supplied 16% of Thailand's total energy needs in 2012 and coal supplied 13% of the country's electrical energy.

In 2011, fuel accounted for 19% of Thailand's imports, the largest single item on the country's import bill (see www.tradingeconomics.com/thailand/imports). As the government is seeking to lower its energy dependence on the rest of the world and reduce carbon dioxide emissions, over the past few years it has promoted ethanol-enhanced gasoline, originally E10 "gasohol", a 10:90 blend of ethanol and petrol, and later added E20, a 20:80 blend. Car companies manufacturing cars in Thailand have cooperated by putting a label on their fuel caps advising drivers to fill up with blended petrol. Consumption of biodiesel production has likewise been promoted.

The Ministry of Energy announced plans in 2013 to increase production of electricity from renewable sources from 2% to 25% of total power within ten years. To further this aim, BOI incentives are available for proposals to manufacture solar cells, alternative energy projects, energy saving equipment in general, and for consulting companies involved with energy-saving projects.

Thailand has also restructured its environmental agency, now the Ministry of Science, Technology and Environment (MOSTE), and has established an environmental fund with a projected annual budget of $80 million. The BOI is actively encouraging investment in clean energy and energy-reduction projects.

Tourism

The World Travel and Tourism Council (www.wttc.org) gathers and collates statistics on tourism for almost all the countries in the world. Countries are ranked by the importance of tourism to their economies (e.g. number of tourists, tourist spending, proportion of tourist dollars to GDP, etc). In 2012 inbound tourism contributed an estimated 7.3% of Thailand's GDP, versus a global average for all countries of 5.2%. Among 189 countries, Thailand ranked 18th in the world in terms of the importance of tourism to its economy.

For tourists who enjoy the city sights, Bangkok is an established vacation destination offering a fusion of cultures from East and West, a full suite of cultural interests, extensive shopping from bargain prices upwards, and nightlife of world renown.

For those who want to relax by the seaside, Thailand has over 3,000 kilometres of sandy tropical beaches. Thailand's three coastlines are the east and west side of the Gulf of Thailand and the shores of the Andaman Sea in the Indian Ocean. Added to these coastal locations are a wide selection of islands off all three coastlines, offering resort-style holiday accommodation from one-star to six-star.

For those who seek a historical experience, standing witness to the country's turbulent past, Thailand has a generous supply of temples, tombs and ancient artefacts, most of them set against a gorgeous landscape.

The Tourist Authority of Thailand (TAT) is the government body promoting tourism in Thailand. In 1999 TAT coined the "Amazing Thailand Always Amazes You" campaign to attract tourists – a highly successful marketing story that has lasted to the present day.

But tourism is by nature a fickle industry, subject to all sorts of positive and negative influences, many beyond the control of the country receiving the tourists. For the past 20 years Thailand has seen a string of events that might have dissuaded tourists from paying a visit. This proved not to be the case. Most of the political disturbances in recent times have been in and around Bangkok. Other than a handful of southern provinces which are a power base of the Democrats, most of rural Thailand has been at peace with itself. One effect of the Bangkok street riots of 2013/14 was not a downturn in tourists visiting Thailand, but a downturn in tourists visiting Bangkok. Tourism into Chiang Mai, Thailand's second city, 700km north of Bangkok, boomed during the period.

The following table suggests that tourism numbers to Amazing Thailand have been amazingly resilient:

Year	Inbound Tourists	Events of Influence
1993	5,770,751	
1994	6,166,795	
1995	6,988,979	
1996	7,188,719	
1997	7,211,369	Asian Financial Crisis
1998	7,772,903	
1999	8,571,569	Millennium bug
2000	9,523,978	
2001	10,060,981	September 11 attacks
2002	10,797,115	
2003	9,864,476	SARS / Bird flu scare in Asia
2004	11,657,629	Tsunami from Aceh earthquake
2005	11.563,459	
2006	13,837,927	Military coup
2007	14,472,490	Government collapses
2008	14,653,374	Yellow Shirts occupy the airport and block roads
2009	14,136,443	Red Shirts riot in the streets
2010	15,810,928	Red Shirts burn down World Trade Bangkok
2011	19,305,056	Floods in Bangkok and central Thailand
2012	22,363,869	Effects of flooding still being felt
2013	26,735,503	Yellow Shirts demonstrate on the streets

Notes: (1) Source of tourist numbers up to 2012 is www.ceicdata.com. This site is downloadable only on subscription. Reported tourist numbers vary between reporting authorities by up to 10%. For example, comparing figures for year 2012, tourist numbers reported by World Travel & Tourism are 21,799,000 and by Tourist Authority of Thailand, 20,051,000. (2) Source for 2013 is Department of Tourism (tourism.go.th/2010/th/statistic/tourismp).

SPECIFIC MARKETS · 39

The table shows that in the 20 years since 1993 tourist number have risen at an average of 7.9% per annum. If this rate of increase is sustained, business enterprises big and small servicing the tourist industry should continue to grow. Thailand's most important source of tourists remains nearby countries in Southeast Asia, as has been the case for a long time. Comparing the nationality profile for incoming tourists over a 15-year period, Taiwan, Hong Kong, Germany and the US have dropped off the list of top ten countries, replaced by Russia, South Korea, Laos and India.

TOP TEN SOURCES OF TOURISTS INTO THAILAND

1998		2013	
1. Japan	12.5%	1. China	17.6%
2. Malaysia	11.7%	2. Malaysia	11.2%
3. Singapore	7.4%	3. Russia	6.5%
4. China	7.2%	4. Japan	5.8%
5. Hong Kong	6.6%	5. South Korea	4.9%
6. Taiwan	5.8%	6. Laos	4.1%
7. Germany	4.8%	7. India	3.9%
8. UK	4.7%	8. Singapore	3.5%
9. USA	4.6%	9. Australia	3.4%
10. Australia	3.8%	10. UK	3.4%

Sources: 1998 figures Immigration Bureau;
2013 figures tourism.go.th

The increase in tourists from China and Russia has more than offset the reduction of tourists from elsewhere, in particular from Europe and the US. Will tourism from China and Russia continue to increase? We know that predicting the future is a hazardous enterprise. Tourism is discretionary spending and therefore one of the first areas to grow in good economic times and shrink when good times turn bad.

It seems to us that a most important factor in future tourist numbers is the growth of an affluent middle class in the source country. China's economy seems to be sustaining its extraordinary rate of growth. Russia has recently passed Saudi Arabia as the

world's number one oil export nation. If these two countries continue to prosper, most likely their tourist numbers will continue
to increase.

Government projects

For information on supplying imported goods and equipment for
Thai government-sponsored projects, companies can register with
the Thai government procurement office (www.goprocurement.
go.th). Information on specific tenders being bid can also be found
at Global Tenders (www.globaltenders.com/login.php), for which
membership is required.

The Prime Minister's Procurement Regulations govern public
sector procurement. These regulations specify non-discriminatory
treatment for all potential bidders. The regulations, however, do
provide preferential treatment for domestic suppliers, who receive
an automatic 15% advantage over foreign bidders in initial-round
bid evaluations. Reports from various studies suggest that award
of government contracts have not been entirely free of corrupt
practices in recent times. Further information on this subject can
be obtained at www.legalink.ch/Root/Sites/legalink/Resources/
Questionnaires/Public-Procurement-Law/Asia/PPL_Thailand.pdf.

From a Thai government viewpoint, sources of goods perceived
as offering high quality include the EEC, North America and Japan.
Emerging economies, like Thailand itself, are not so highly regarded.
For example, in the case of the Petroleum Authority of Thailand
(PTT), the Thai government oil company, equipment made from
steel sourced from places like China, Eastern Europe and South
America is specifically excluded in PTT's conditions of purchase.

At least at the official level, this is likely to change. With the
entry of Thailand into Asean Economic Community in 2015, Thailand, like other countries, will have to rewrite their trading rules.
Since free trade between members will be a fundamental principle
of the AEC, restrictions of Thai government entities against goods
from places like Cambodia and Myanmar will have to be eased,
and relations with countries outside ASEAN standardised across
the association.

Agriculture

Rice is the mainstay of Thai agriculture. Much of the rice grown in Thailand is for domestic consumption but sufficient surplus remains to make Thailand the world's top rice-exporting nation.

However, Thailand's rice economy suffered a setback in recent years. In 2011 the incoming Thai government honoured an election promise to buy rice in unlimited quantities from its farmers at up to 50% over the market price (the "rice pledge"). At the time, rice production from the world's second biggest rice exporter, Vietnam, had suffered due to an unseasonal heat wave in 2010. But for the following two years, countries around Asia, including Thailand, enjoyed bumper rice harvests. In addition, a great deal of rice flowed into Thailand from farmers in neighbouring countries, in particular from Cambodia, to cash in on the Thai government's rice subsidy. As a result, about 18 million tons of surplus rice has accumulated in Thailand's warehouses, which, at time of writing, are full to capacity.

Negative spin-off effects from the rice subsidy scheme are farmers disgruntled at the prospect of having their subsidy removed, an unwanted mountain of rice with a use-by date of about a year filling the country's warehouses, corruption allegations involving the prime minister and a possible downgrading of the country's sovereign debt rating due to the unfunded US$5 billion government obligation so far incurred to rice farmers.

Rubber, Thailand's second most important crop, is faring only slightly better than rice in world markets. In 2012 the Thai government announced a scheme to help rubber farmers by buying rubber at premium prices in a world market, which, like rice, was oversupplied. But unlike rice, rubber can more easily be stored and is an important raw material to industry, in particular the auto industry, which has the capacity to absorb surpluses locally, given sufficient time.

Farming is top of FBA's list of industries off limits to foreigners. For economic, social and political reasons, the government intends to keep ownership and operations of the rural landscape much the same as they have been for centuries. In recent years, the productivity of the rural sector has risen with increased mechanisation, improved crop genetics and wider use of fertilisers, herbicides and insecticides. Though rural employment declines each year with population drift to cities, agricultural output has risen slightly.

Processing Thai agricultural products, such as canning pineapples and other fruit, rather than growing crops, probably presents the best opportunity for investors in the agricultural sector.

Construction

After recovering from a general market downturn in 2008, construction in Thailand was affected by the 2011 floods, growing by only 2.3% over the previous year. However, the industry was back on track in 2012, growing at 7.6% per annum. At time of writing, growth at about this rate is expected to continue for another couple of years (see, for example, www.researchonglobalmarkets. com).

The construction industry is on the FBA's List 3 as not normally available to 100% foreign-owned firms, but can be joint ventured with a Thai partner. Except for specialist major projects offering unique engineering challenges, construction opportunities for foreigners in Thailand are likely to be limited. Thai construction companies on large projects like high-rise buildings are already operating in the country. Construction technology transfer to Thai companies has largely already occurred.

Most of Thailand's infrastructure is owned and operated by the government. Projects for major infrastructure projects are let by tender, sometimes to local firms, sometimes to overseas firms and sometimes to consortia of both, depending on the nature of the project and the government's rules on tendering. For large-scale construction, the best opportunities for foreigners in Thailand are for specialist infrastructure projects.

The other sector of the construction market where foreigners operate is housing construction on a small scale. Rules governing building companies and developers vary with locality and types of structures. Builders of condominiums must hold a building licence and may be subject to inspections. House builders in Bangkok and major towns and cities have to work with local authorities, submit building plans and obtain permits in the name of either the Thai partner or the juristic person in which the Thai partner owns a 51% or better stake.

Rules in provinces are more relaxed and vary from one place to the next. For small developments of plots up to eight houses, developers in rural districts typically don't need to submit building plans to authorities, aren't subject to building inspections, and don't need to acquire certificates of occupancy. In addition there is no requirement for qualified tradesmen. As a result many unqualified foreigners get into small-scale developments and building activities in Thailand, usually in association with Thai partners.

Retail

Thailand's promotion from lower-middle-income economy to higher-middle-income economy (as per the World Bank definition) indicates a growing middle class with cash to spend. However, encouraging foreigners to participate in retailing has not been part of the government's agenda to develop the Thai economy.

The Foreign Business Act restricts 100% foreign ownership of retail outlets to companies capitalised over 100 million baht. Even for companies of this size, foreigners have pretty much pulled out of large retail operations such as megamalls and hypermarkets. The three biggest supermarket chains in Thailand are Carrefour, Tesco-Lotus, and Makro Foods. All three had their origins in Europe – Carrefour in France, Tesco in Britain, and Makro in Holland. All three now have Thai owners. Thai company Big C has taken over and rebranded Carrefour stores in Thailand. Charoen Pokphand Foods – more commonly called CP – owns both Tesco and Makro outlets. CP is also the franchisor for Thailand's ubiquitous 7/11 outlets, located on every second street corner.

In 2006 the Ministry of Commerce announced its intention to implement a Retailing Act to restrict the power of supermarkets and hypermarkets that were seen to be undermining family-run retail businesses. Shortly after a bill to this effect was presented to Parliament, but before it was passed, the army removed the sitting government and the idea lapsed. At the time this book went to print the bill for the mooted Retailing Act had not been represented to Parliament.

The best opportunities for foreigners retailing in Thailand are high-end-brand stores such as Cartier, Prada and Dior. By contrast, retailing from small stores is difficult for foreigners due to work permit restrictions and the need to interact with customers in Thai. In addition, trying to compete with Thai-dominated industries tends to attract the notice of owners of competitive Thai stores who only have to file a complaint to have government inspectors visit and find some fault with a foreign-owned store. The alternative for foreigners who wish to establish retail operations in Thailand is as passive investors. In this case, foreigners would not seek to obtain work permits for themselves and thereby avoid the requirement to employ Thai staff. Instead they would allow their Thai partners to run the business.

Entrepreneurial street life

The entrepreneurial spirit is alive and well on the streets of Thailand. Thais are not stay-at-home people. They like to fraternise with others in a common space, which in Thai towns and cities is usually the street. As can be judged from the number of noodle stands set up on footpaths in every city and town in the country, not only are Thais entrepreneurial at the individual level, but the local authorities have a relaxed attitude to their activities. Studies by the International Labour Office (ILO) and others have found that a substantial percentage of the community are stakeholders in street-vending activities, particularly of food. In 2000, according to an ILO study, the community was eating 50% of its evening meals on the street, and the casual food industry was providing direct employment to nearly half a million people in the lower socio-economic groups. Shop owners and restaurateurs would like to close down street vendors, but they are massively outnumbered by both the street vendors (who get their on-street premises rent-free) and their customers (who get their meals at bargain prices).

We recognise that foreign small-business people are unlikely to engage directly in street vending. But operating bars, the next level up the catering food chain, is one of the most common activities for small-scale foreign entrepreneurs in Thailand. Bar owners interact with street vendors on the day-to-day level. A lot of them source their cooked food off the street then resell it, probably at a mark-up, to their customers.

Foreigners in small businesses in Thailand are bound by the same rules as businesses of any size, plus other rules associated with long-term visas and work permits for themselves. Often they may involve themselves in businesses such as selling food and drink that are not on the government's preferred list of business activities. In general they are compelled to form 49/51% owned ventures of one type or another.

Many come to Thailand for lifestyle reasons: some are men setting up a life with their Thai partner, others are attracted to the low cost of living, others come for the weather. When they get here, these small-time entrepreneurs need something to keep themselves or their partners occupied.

Bars, food outlets and massage parlours owned by foreigners associated with Thai partners are generally thought to have a high failure rate, though no statistics are available. There are all sorts of reasons why such ventures fail. Often, foreign investors have no experience in their chosen industry. Under the regulations, their capital requirements are most likely higher than Thai competitors operating a bar up the street. Their Thai partners may exploit them. They may not be able to establish friendly relations with the police. They may lack the contacts to source their inputs at minimum cost. Compliance with the Alien Working Act may cripple their business by obliging them to employ more Thais than their business justifies. And if, despite the foregoing, they are making a good living, the local up the street in the same line of business may complain to the authorities about some real or imagined rule infraction that might result in their enterprise shutting down.

It is possible for foreign owners of small retail businesses to make a living in Thailand, but they do have to work within or around thickets of rules and regulations backed up with stern penalties for those caught transgressing.

Education

To satisfy the policy objective first declared in the 1950s to turn itself from an agriculture society into a highly industrialised economy, Thailand saw the need to educate a skilled workforce.

Over the past couple of decades, recognised overseas institutes of learning have moved into Thailand in large numbers. In 1992 there were three international schools in Thailand. By 1998 this had risen to 45. By 2013, 164 international schools and 202 institutes of higher education – many of them branches of first-world universities and colleges – were at work in the country educating the future workforce.

Education also presents opportunities for foreign entrepreneurs of more modest means. One of the ways foreigners can stay in Thailand is on student visas, renewable for up to three years. No rigorous course of study in any particular discipline is required to validate student visas. Many foreigners in Thailand on student visas legitimise their long-term residency rights by taking courses in Thai on a more or less permanent basis.

Language schools with enrolments from a handful to hundreds are widespread through Thailand. These schools offer their operators a number of revenue streams. Typically courses teaching Thai to foreigners run for 8–10 weeks with class-work of four hours per week, after which students sit a marked exam set by the school. The school sends exam results to the Immigration Department, and for a fee provided by students, organises visa extensions. Students don't need to pass their exams to earn an extension to their student visas. They just need to show up to class at exam time, submit a paper and be awarded a mark higher than zero. By continuing their Thai studies and sitting regular exams, students can earn yearly visa extensions for a maximum stay of three to five years. Language schools also obtain enrolments from foreigners with retirement visas who wish to learn Thai. A third possible revenue stream for a language school is Thais wishing to improve their

English. But extending the visas of foreign students is the main revenue centre, with about 70% of revenue typically from this source. Fees are around 3,000 baht per student for a course of 8–10 weeks.

Most of the courses offered by language schools in Thailand teach foreigners to speak and/or write Thai from English, but some schools also run classes teaching Thai from other languages such as German and French. Another option for both investors and foreigners seeking work is to use foreigners to teach Thai students the native language of the foreigner. A number of English as a Second Language (ESL) schools as well as a nationwide network of franchised TEFL (Teaching English as a Foreign Language) schools operate in the kingdom. (For lists of these schools, see www.esl-base.com/school/Thailand and www.teflcourse.net.)

As with all other businesses in Thailand, foreigners investing in schools require Thai partners. A language school also requires a licence issued by the Ministry of Education (www.moe.go.th) in the area local to the proposed school. Restrictions on nationality of personnel are that the principal and director of the school must be Thai. But there are no stipulations regarding nationality or educational standards of teachers. Work permits for native English-speaking teachers are relatively easy to get since this is considered a job opportunity that can't readily be filled by Thais and also because the government wants its population to speak English as a second language.

Foreigners wishing to stay in Thailand to teach English as a second language can obtain information on teaching opportunities in Thailand at the Ajarn.com teacher recruitment website.

Trading blocs and future markets

Thailand is geographically positioned in the hub of Southeast Asia. Clockwise from the north, countries with which Thailand shares its land borders are Myanmar (formerly Burma), Laos, Cambodia and Malaysia. Its slightly less immediate neighbours include China, Vietnam, Singapore and Indonesia. The large populations of neighbouring countries are prospective markets for businesses establishing in Thailand.

Thailand is a member of at least nine trade associations with other countries in the region and beyond. Trade agreements allowing investors from member countries to take advantage of a variety of investment and trade concessions are specific to each treaty.

The full list of treaties to which Thailand is a signatory, along with the text of the treaties in English, can be found at the Department of Foreign Trade (www.dft.go.th/Default.aspx?tabid=372). Highlights of the three trade agreements most likely to be of interest to foreign investors are described below.

Association of South East Asian Nations (ASEAN)
In 1967, to obtain the benefits of mutual trade and to form a bastion against the spread of communism into the region, Thailand, the Philippines, Indonesia, Singapore and Malaysia formed ASEAN (the Association of South East Asian Nations). Since then, ASEAN membership has expanded to include Laos, Vietnam, Cambodia, Brunei and latterly, Myanmar.

In 2015 ASEAN is scheduled to widen its horizons further by becoming AEC (ASEAN Economic Community), modelled on the European Economic Community, but without a common currency. Like the EEC, the objectives of the AEC are to promote trade and economic efficiency between member states by lowering trade barriers.

The AEC Economic Blueprint, written in English and signed in 2007 by leaders of participating countries, identifies the objectives of the AEC (see www.asean.org/archive/5187-10.pdf). A particular statement from Section 4 that might strike a chord with prospective foreign investors in Thailand states: "The leaders agreed ... to transform ASEAN into a region with free movement of goods, services, investment, skilled labour, and freer flow of capital."

We note that implementing these objectives will require a major rewriting of Thailand's laws, the main purpose of which, as we describe elsewhere in this book, has been to do just the opposite, that is, to restrict the free movement of goods, investment, labour and capital and thereby ensure that Thais would remain the owners of their realm. Further into the text of the AEC blueprint, "free movement of goods" is defined to mean zero tariffs, stand-ardisation of customs procedures and elimination of non-tariff barriers throughout member states.

With the AEC about to come into force, Thailand's relations with neighbouring countries Cambodia and Myanmar may need a makeover. Thais are still in dispute with the Cambodians over title to Preah Vihear temple, located in the Dangrek Mountains, on the Thai-Cambodian border. After scrutiny of various treaties since 1767, in 1911 a panel of international jurists found the temple to be in Cambodian territory. This finding failed to settle the matter for Thais. The last skirmish between Thai and Cambodian armies for title to the temple was in 2011. Pending further negotiations, a ceasefire agreed to place the temple in no man's land but under Cambodian control. At time of writing, this is the current status.

So far as Myanmar is concerned, there are about 150,000 refugees on the Thai-Myanmar border who at present have no legal right to employment in Thailand, but have no desire to return to Myanmar. Largely they find unofficial work in Thailand, where they have no rights and tend to be exploited. The status of these displaced people needs to resolved.

The AEC Economic Blueprint prescribes a timetable for 2008 to 2020 for standardising laws relating to labour, foreign trade, capital requirements and economic activity. Whether Thailand's Parliament can pass legislation to meet its AEC commitments has yet to be seen. If it does, Thailand's rules on investment, labour and capital for investors from ASEAN countries will be greatly eased and rules for investors from countries outside ASEAN will be standardised across all ASEAN member states.

If it doesn't, rules will stay the same as they are now.

This book describes the rules in force at time of writing.

Indian Ocean Rim (IOR)

Thailand is a member of the IOR economic co-operative to promote trade and investment for member countries encircling the Indian Ocean. IOR has a total of 20 member states on three continents (Australia, Africa and Asia) and six dialogue partners.

Asia-Pacific Economic Cooperation (APEC)
APEC is a broader-based trading group comprising all the ASEAN members plus other countries around the Pacific, including Japan, Korea, Canada, Hong Kong, Chinese Taipei, China, Papua New Guinea, Peru, Russia, Chile, the United States, Mexico, Australia and New Zealand. APEC's 21 member countries hope to achieve free and open trade, investment and technical cooperation throughout the region by the year 2020.

Chapter 4

Importing and Exporting

Individuals and companies interested in exporting goods from their home country into Thailand can either establish a branch office in Thailand or appoint a Thai distributor. Since all countries are anxious to export, an initial source of export advice is the home country's Department of Trade or equivalent – advice that is generally provided free of charge.

Since laws governing the rights and obligations of foreign entrepreneurs and their Thai business associates are intricate and detailed, we suggest you use a Thai lawyer before signing any agreements with your intended Thai distributor.

After you have appointed a distributor, frequent follow-up visits are a good idea. Once appointed, your Thai agent will most likely want to take you to see his major customers. Face-to-face contact is important in Thailand and about the best way possible to promote your goods.

Product documentation

Few brochures for technical and engineering products are translated into Thai; those that are translated from English into Thai are dotted with English technical words which have no equivalents in Thai. If your product comes with operating and maintenance instructions, you might get away with English only, but an accompanying Thai translation would be helpful. If you are selling highly technical goods, such as engineering and construction equipment, you can probably do much of your business in English.

For retail goods, however, you will need packaging in Thai, or a combination of English and Thai. At a minimum, a stick-on label in Thai over the English label is required. Sales brochures for consumer products should normally be in Thai.

An important point for those from the English-speaking West to observe in Thailand is the reluctance of Thais to ask questions that might display the questioner's ignorance. You can be almost sure that if your import agent does not understand your brochure, you won't receive an e-mail asking you to explain it. To establish whether your import agent really understands the finer points of your product, you will need to determine the extent of your agent's product knowledge during a personal visit.

Import documentation

In Thailand, like most places, importing procedures are best conducted by people familiar with the country's rules, that is to say, import agents. However we will make a few observations here to help those intrepid souls who intend to manage their own Customs clearances.

To take advantage of the efficiencies of the electronic age, the Thai Customs Department now works through a computerised system – e-Import – though which the standard shipping documents long associated with importing – packing lists, bills of lading and import declarations – are submitted electronically.

There was a time when some greasing of palms was thought to expedite customs clearance of goods imported into Thailand. One of the advantages of the electronic age to suppliers is that Customs officers may find it more difficult to delay paperwork while hanging out for a bribe.

Some people claim that paperwork processing may be expedited if the documents are translated into Thai. However, English is very much the language of commerce in Thailand and translation errors between the two languages are always possible. Besides, shipping documents are mostly prepared in the originating country where Thai speakers are likely to be thin on the ground, and writers of Thai even more so. English-language documentation usually gets the job done.

Details of obligations to importers and payment of taxes and surcharges can be obtained from the Thai Customs website. Payment of duty is by electronic transfer. Landing, handling and storage charges will also be incurred and must be paid before goods can be collected. To effect these transactions, if you are establishing a branch in Thailand, you will need to set up a Thai bank account in advance of importing goods into the country.

One point we might note is that Customs won't notify you when your shipment arrives. Your import agent, if you have one, will keep tabs on your affairs. Failing that, the shipper can provide shipping details and likely location of your shipment. Assuming your documentation is complete, your goods should clear in two to three days. Like most other places, leaving goods to languish in Customs warehouses is likely to attract substantial demurrage charges.

Tariffs

Imports into Thailand require an import licence detailed down to individual items being imported. Tariffs are assessed on the value of imported goods at rates which vary between one category of goods and another. Knowledge of the scale of tariffs applying to particular category may save you money if you can arrange things to include your goods in a category attracting the minimum tariff.

Imports are also subject to sales tax (VAT), currently charged at 7% on CIF value (Cost, Insurance & Freight) plus duty. In addition, imports may incur excise and other surcharges depending on their nature. Details of rates of duty, excise and surcharges on specific items can be obtained from Thai Customs (customs_clinic@ customs.go.th or call-centre tel: 1164). The general principle is that goods of strategic importance to Thailand, or goods required to manufacture products for re-export, are free of tariffs and taxes. These goods may either enter the country tax- and tariff-free, or may incur taxes and tariffs on arrival, and are later reimbursed.

Prohibited goods and restricted goods

Acts of Parliament that restrict or prohibit the import and export of specific classes of goods in Thailand are the Customs Act and the Export and Import of Goods Act.

Two categories of goods are distinguished under these acts: Prohibited Goods, which are not allowed either to enter or leave the country; and Restricted Goods, whose movement across national borders requires permits from a Thai government agency. Since the list of prohibited and restricted imports is frequently updated, it will be worth checking with the Customs Department before arranging to import or export your products for the first time.

Typical of prohibited imports are pornographic material, objects impugning Thai national symbols, drugs, pirated software, certain chemicals and many foodstuffs. Restricted goods include works of art, living species, firearms and pharmaceutical products requiring approval of health authorities.

As has been much publicised by photographs of captured drug runners sitting behind their haul of drugs, importing prohibited goods into Thailand can earn stiff penalties. Both the Customs Act and the Export and Import of Goods Act prescribe a maximum of ten years' imprisonment and fines of up to five times the value of the goods for serious infractions.

In addition, Section 20 of the Export and Import of Goods Act details the rights and entitlements of informants to a share of the spoils in the event a penalty is imposed for violating the act. This provision, it seems to us, would encourage officers of the Department of Customs to discharge their duties with the utmost diligence and likewise encourage a disgruntled employee of the enterprise to provide whatever help these conscientious officers require!

Temporary entry

Products for exhibitions or demonstrations can be imported for up to six months without payment of custom duties and value-added tax. Businesses must obtain a bank guarantee for the value of the imports. If the products are not re-exported within six months, the bank guarantee will be exercised by the Department of Customs for duties and tax payable.

Customs valuation

As a general principle, valuation of goods subject to tariffs is determined by the World Trade Organisation (WTO) Valuation System to standardise valuation methods world-wide. The objective of these rules is to set a basis of valuation that is fair to both importing and exporting nations. Subject to qualifications and adjustments allowed by various different valuation methods allowed under WTO rules, the basic value is the CIF invoice value of goods on shipping documents. However, Thai Customs allows itself a wide scope for argument on the valuation figure by using alternative methods of valuation, such as comparison with the sale price of similar items within Thailand. Those interested in exploring this subject in greater depth can refer to a discussion on the determination of "transaction value" by Thai Customs Department at their website (www2.customs.go.th/Customs-Eng/Valuation) and to the WTO webpage on this topic (www.wto.org/english/tratop_e/cusval_e/cusval_info_e.htm). Should a dispute arise between an importer and Thai Customs, the importer is entitled to file an appeal against a Customs Department valuation within 30 days of receiving a Valuation Notification of the goods.

Import quotas

Import quotas are designed to protect local suppliers and, in the case of goods involving national strategic objectives, to avoid relying on a foreign power for a vital resource. However, to further its globalisation objectives, the WTO exerts relentless pressure to reduce or eliminate quotas world-wide whatever the nature of the goods being supplied. Additional pressure on quotas has been applied by Thailand's trading partners, in particular China.

A local producer competing against imports subject to import quotas faces a long-term risk that, at the stroke of pen, bureaucracy can change the rules, thereby suddenly exposing the local (Thai) producer to international competition from the world market. This factor should be considered when evaluating projects in Thailand to produce goods on the import quota list.

Importing foodstuffs

Importing foodstuffs presents special difficulties. The Thai law on food is the Food Act of BE 2522 (1979) and its amendments. Firms importing foods must be licensed with the Thai Food and Drug Agency (www.fda.moph.go.th/eng), a department of the Ministry of Health. The rules on food importing are far too complicated to be described in this book. The best English-language reference we found on the subject is the USDA's report "Thailand: Food and Agricultural Import Regulations and Standards". Subjects covered in the report include import licensing requirements, Thai monitoring authorities, import permits, food additive regulations, pesticide levels, contaminants, shelf life, testing and quality control requirements and labelling rules, packaging regulations, prohibited foods and substances, required certifications, control of food advertising and trademark regulations. (The full report is found on the USDA Gain website: gain.fas.usda.gov.)

At time of writing, Thailand has imposed import quotas on 23 agricultural products. These are lychees, coconut pulp, milk, butter, potatoes, onion, garlic, coconut, coffee, tea, dried capsicum, corn, rice, bean, onion seeds, bean oil, bean cake, sugar cane, coconut oil, palm oil, instant coffee, local tobacco slices, and silk. Since listed items change from time to time, prospective importers of agricultural products are advised to check the list frequently to see what's been added/deleted.

Export finance and insurance

Thailand set up the government owned Export-Import Bank (Exim Thailand) under an Act of Parliament (Export-Import Bank Act of 1993). Its mission was, and still is, to stimulate exports out of Thailand and assist imports into Thailand of strategic products. Another objective of the bank is to assist Thai businesses become more competitive in overseas markets. To further these objectives the bank provides financial assistance to trading entities on both sides of its national borders. For foreigners considering Thailand as an investment destination, services the bank provides that might be of interest are:

- Provision of credit facilities for the exporter's bank, for the exporter, for the importer's bank and for the importer
- Provision of credit facilities for importing goods or services or for manufacturing goods for export for firms other than importers and exporters
- Provision of export credit and insurance services, outside those currently available at commercial banks
- Raising business finance
- Provision of financial advisory services
- Provision of information and consulting services on export and business opportunities in countries which are target markets for products of the business

Potential investors interested in obtaining details of these services can check the EXIM Thailand website (www.exim.go.th).

Chapter 5

Establishing the Business

There is no law preventing foreigners from registering a company without Thai business partners. But having done so there are severe restrictions on what the company can do without obtaining an Alien Business Licence (ABL), which is only granted for a very restricted range of business activities, in particular specialist manufacturing.

Outside those activities, you will need a Thai partner.

Finding a partner

For foreign firms seeking a joint-venture partner, a possible source of Thai contacts is the Board of Investment, which holds country-to-country fairs and other industry events that are usually well patronised (see www.thaitradefair.com). The Chamber of Commerce in your own country is also a lead worth pursuing before arriving in Thailand. Likewise, governments of most source countries have departments that will provide assistance for citizens heading overseas to develop business links with other countries.

In Bangkok, organisations that hold regular networking events are Bangkok Networking Community, BNI Inspire, the Foreign Correspondents Club of Thailand and Thailand Direct Networking. Embassies of your own countries in Thailand are also likely to host networking sessions.

Should you have no initial leads, websites of introductory agencies, such as thaitrade.com, can advise you of firms in Thailand that might be interested in distributing your product or entering into joint-venture agreements. (See, for example, www.globaltrade.net/ m/c/agent-distributors/Thailand.html.) For those wishing to export goods to Thailand made in their home countries, potential Thai importer agents listed by product can be found at www.alibaba. com/countrysearch/TH/importer-list.html.

Business arrangements in Thailand

Company structures in Thailand are similar to those in the West. The first step is to create what Thai law refers to as a "juristic person", which is much the same as a registered company in Western parlance, with similar rights to conduct business in its own name, enter contracts, sign leases and employ a workforce. As previously noted, the Amity Treaty between the US and Thailand may relieve Americans from many of the obligations imposed by the FBA on foreigners of other nationalities.

Company structure options for investors establishing a base in Thailand are as follows:

- Sole proprietorship
- Partnership
  - Ordinary partnership
  - Limited partnership
- Limited company
  - Closely held company
  - Publicly held company
- Branch of a foreign-owned business
- Representative office

A sole proprietorship, under the ownership of one individual, is unlikely to be practicable for a foreigner setting up business in Thailand due to FBA rules on Thai shareholdings, unless he or she is prepared to prepared to hand over all aspects of the business, including the capital requirements, to a Thai national. In that case, in the absence of a work permit, the foreign investor must be prepared to play no part in running the business. The foreign investor is putting his entire trust in his Thai partner. Many high-risk small businesses such as bars and restaurants are run on this basis. Regarding such arrangements we can only repeat the advice of acquaintances who've tried it: the odds are against you.

As in the West, partnerships in Thailand do not enjoy the limited liability of limited companies. For ordinary partnerships all partners have unlimited liability for the activities of other partners. In limited partnerships, junior partners do enjoy limited liability, however the managing partner has unlimited liability. As in other places in the world, partnerships are most common to particular activities, such as legal and accounting services.

A limited company of private shareholders is the most common corporate arrangement for foreign entrepreneurs investing in Thailand.

Publicly listing limited liability companies such as IPOs are out of range for all but very large companies.

Branches of 100% foreign owned businesses are restricted to a few industries, in particular to large foreign manufacturers such as auto companies or computer companies and their specialist component suppliers.

Representative offices can be established on a temporary basis (five years maximum) while companies assess their prospects for setting up permanent operations in Thailand. Representative offices are precluded from engaging in commercial (profit-making) activities.

Joint ventures

Foreign/Thai Joint Ventures are by far the most common corporate structures under which foreigners do business in Thailand. Rules on the shareholdings of Thai/foreign joint ventures are defined under the FBA. Joint ventures are typically limited companies of private shareholders, with a share allocation arrangement between two or more companies, between individuals, or between a mix of companies and individuals.

Thais are accustomed to the idea of joint venturing with foreign partners. In fact many Thai firms actively seek joint-venture partners to bring technical, technological, marketing, and management skills to their businesses. In return, Thai partners may offer local language skills, familiarity with local business conditions, contacts with the local business community, and the ability to liaise with government officials, customers, suppliers and Thai staff. They may, or may not, contribute to the capital of the business.

Other than for citizens and corporations covered under the Amity Treaty with the US, the most common ownership arrangement is that Thai joint venture partners own a minimum of 51% of the shares of a Thai/foreign enterprise. The minimum *number* of shareholders is seven. In addition the board of the company must have a majority of Thai directors.

This arrangement has an implied assumption that 51% of the share ownership holds 51% of the voting power. However, the FBA as presently written isn't specific about the connection between share ownership and voting rights. It is commonly believed (though we understand it hasn't been tested in a Thai court) that the law as written allows the foreign partner to retain decision-making powers for the entity by issuing two classes of shares – 49% to the foreigner with full voting rights and 51% to the Thai shareholders with diminished voting rights. This loophole would have been closed by an amendment to the Foreign Business Act drafted in 2007, but before it was promulgated there was a change in government, after which the amendment was abandoned. As a result, at the time of writing we understand that issuing two classes of shares with different voting entitlements is probably still legal.

The idea of joint venturing as juristic persons is well accepted in Thailand and has percolated down to the smallest businesses. One particular entitlement of a Thai juristic person (an entity whose definition includes a 51Thai/49Foreign Joint Venture) is the entitlement to own land. Foreign house-owners in Thailand customarily enter an arrangement between themselves and one or more Thai nationals to create a 51% Thai-owned juristic person from whom to lease back the land on which their house is built – commonly on a 30-year lease with the option of 30-year extensions. This generally works to the satisfaction of all stakeholders as long as the lessee wishes to continue the arrangement. However, problems may arise when, for example, a foreign lessee wishes to sell his house built on land leased from the Thai juristic person as lessor, and the lessor decides against assigning the lease to the new lessee (i.e. the potential buyer of the house). In such a case the house-owner may be precluded from selling the house because he/she doesn't own the land on which it has been built.

Selecting the right Thai partners may be the most important decision in ensuring the success of a new foreign/Thai joint venture business. Like hiring a CEO, it's worth spending plenty of time and effort finding the individual or corporate venture partner best suited to your needs. The more your partner contributes, the better the chances of success.

Capital requirements

For small businesses employing ten or fewer foreigners, the Foreign Business Act requires that the minimum initial capital to establish a joint venture in Thailand is 2 million baht for each foreigner working in the business. This capital is almost always subscribed by the foreign partner. For larger businesses that have been trading for a few years, rules relating to the hiring of foreigners get a little more complicated, with entitlements to hire foreigners being related to the amount of taxes the business is paying as well as to the capital invested.

Registration procedures also require the joint venture to obtain a work permit for the foreign partner. Since the number of Thai workers the firm is obliged to employ is determined by the number of work permits issued, whatever role the foreign partner performs in the business, the capital requirements of the business and the minimum number of Thai staff on the payroll will be based on at least one foreign employee. Therefore the minimum capital investment of a foreign/Thai joint venture is two million baht unless the Thai partner is running the show and the foreign partner is merely a passive investor. Under the passive investor arrangement, as well as not being able to work in the business, the foreign partner cannot be a director since foreign directors require work permits.

The meaning of "capital" in terms of the FBA provisions is not entirely clear. The most liberal interpretation is that capital might be regarded in the Western sense as "authorised capital" (i.e. not necessarily fully paid up). But the more widely accepted interpretation is that two million baht cash per work permit is required.

However, there may be loopholes in this area of law. Some advisors suggest that a way around fully subscribing the two million baht bottom limit is to show the capital as a book entry and then lend part of it back to the foreign proprietor as a loan. We are not sure how legal this is, or whether it's ever been tested. If money is short, it may be worth checking this point with a Thai lawyer prior to registering the business. Whatever the result, the FBA does require that 25% of the registered capital be paid in cash or kind within three months of the company's incorporation.

To incorporate, company registration forms can be downloaded from the Ministry of Commerce's Department of Business Development (www.dbd.go.th). In addition, within 60 days of commencement of trading, the company must apply to the Revenue Department (www.rd.go.th) for a corporate tax ID number. Ventures in the entertainment industry (e.g. restaurants, massage parlours, dance venues) also require an entertainment licence and, if applicable, an alcohol licence from the local district police office.

An additional obligation, depending on the nature of the business, is that the venture is obliged to employ four Thai workers for every work permit issued to a foreigner. Since for very small one-or two-person businesses, employment at the prescribed level may be burdensome, some foreign entrepreneurs try to find a way round the rules by employing "phantom" employees – real people who are registered employees but do not work in the business and are not paid. Since tax records are kept for each employee, if this dubious course of adopted, taxes assessed on the imaginary earnings of phantoms must still be paid.

To register the company with the Ministry of Commerce, a Memorandum of Association must be prepared with the following information:

- Name and address of the company
- Objectives of the company
- Registered capital and details of issued shares
- Names, addresses and nationalities of shareholders
- Names and addresses of directors

As in the West, it pays to define your business objectives as widely as possible in the Memorandum of Association, so the business can head off in whatever direction its future dictates without having to redefine its intentions. As a side note, the Ministry of Commerce provides a Standard Memorandum of Association with objectives wide-ranging enough to cover most business activities. Use of this form is thought to speed up the registration process with the ministry.

Legal system

For the convenience of potential foreign investors, English translations of most of the laws relating to establishing a business in Thailand – customs laws, labour laws, government assistance packages to selected industries, payment of taxes, banking and rules regarding the purchase of land, etc – can be downloaded from the internet by typing in the name of the particular act (in English).

On the other hand, the legal system in Thailand recognises Thai as the operating language. If you originate your contracts in English you will need to have them translated into Thai for contracts to carry weight in a Thai court. In addition, to be legally binding, stamp duty is payable on most contracts and leases at a rate specified in the Duty Stamp Schedule of the Revenue Code (www.rd.go.th/publish/37773.0.html). Normally the contract or lease must have a duty stamp attached at its time of execution. Contracting parties resident outside Thailand are given 30 days to get the stamp attached to their contracts.

Broadly speaking, civil disputes, such as enforcing property or contract rights, are resolved through Thai courts in a similar manner to other countries. In the event of translation errors between English and Thai versions of the contract, the Thai version will prevail, even if the contract was written in English in the first place. At present Thailand is not a member of the International Centre for the Settlement of Investment Disputes. Foreigners in Thailand may not enforce a judgement that has been adjudicated in a foreign country. For a dispute between Thais and foreigners to be enforced in Thailand, new proceedings must be initiated in Thailand.

Using a lawyer

As anywhere, lawyers cost money, though fees of Thai lawyers are nothing like as ferocious as the West. Those who have aversion to using lawyers should note that learning the ins and outs of local laws in a foreign land and in a difficult foreign language presents stern challenges. Much of the paperwork a foreigner might complete under his or her own steam back in the home country might, in Thailand, be better done with the assistance of a lawyer. Lawyers can advise on the various types of business arrangements that comply with local laws, register firms, obtain requisite permits, advise on options for leasing company premises, advise on labour laws, help register patents and trademarks, and take other legal steps to protect a product from intellectual property rights infringement. There is no shortage of competent English-speaking lawyers in Thailand – both Thai and foreign. Should you decide that hiring a lawyer is worth investigating, one place you can start your search for legal assistance is the Thai Law Forum (www.thailawforum.com/lawyer.html).

Interacting with bureaucrats

For expats visiting Thailand, only short-stay tourists will avoid significant interaction with the Thai bureaucracy. If you stay and work in Thailand, a large number of documents will be presented for your signature. You will also find that the Thai bureaucracy has an insatiable appetite for your passport photograph. It's worth assembling a supply of photographs in three different sizes to affix to documents, since Thai government departments have yet to standardise size specifications for photos.

Visas

Tourists to Thailand from most countries can obtain 30-day tourist visas on entry at the airport. Foreign entrepreneurs entering the country to check out conditions can do so on a tourist visa provided they are not classed as working while in the country.

But once you have decided to set up your own business in Thailand, you need the paperwork to extend your sojourn in Thailand beyond 30 days. At that point the paperwork requirements increase substantially.

If you have come to the country on a tourist visa, you will need to return to home base and obtain a non-immigrant visa from the Thai consulate in your own country. Non-immigrant visas come in 12 different flavours designated by a letter, of which only one relates to employment. This is the "Non-Immigrant B" ("B" for business) visa that allows you to stay in Thailand for 90 days while you set up your company and organise your work permit. The Non-Immigrant B visa can either be for single entry into Thailand for 90 days, or multiple entries for a year. Preferably those setting up business in Thailand should get a multiple re-entry visa that renews its 90 days entitlement every time you leave and re-enter the country. Alternatively if you don't travel out of the country during the year of your visa, 15 days either side of the expiry date of your 90 day entitlement, you can visit the Bureau of Immigration to seek an extension for a further 90 days. Within 15 days of the expiry date of the visa itself you need to obtain another visa. Unlike the initial visa, the renewed Non-Immigrant B visa can be obtained within Thailand at the Immigration Bureau.

If you happen to make a trip outside the country from which you return just before your visa is due to expire, the 90 day extension on your visa will still start from the date you return. In effect this turns a 12-month visa into a 15-month visa.

The most common form-filling venues for visitors to and foreign residents in Thailand is the Immigration Bureau (alternatively called the Immigration Department). The person you are dealing with at Immigration will be dressed in a uniform and sit at a wooden desk strewn with papers. That Thailand spends a relatively small proportion of its GNP on government services does not indicate a shortage of officials to process paperwork. Rather it indicates that the vast army of petty Thai government bureaucrats processing visa and permit applications are poorly paid, and might wish to earn whatever supplementary income becomes available to them during the course of their employment.

If you meet the requirements for extending your visa, well and good. You pay a small fee stipulated by the government and you're on your way. But if there is some irregularity with your visa-extension paperwork, it's time to call in an expert. Usually persons with expertise in these matters can be found plying their trade outside the immigration office. They are Thais, not in uniform, asking if they can help visa-seeking farangs whose initial offerings have been rejected and are wandering around, pondering their next move.

If you are a recent addition to the list of rejects, you can explain your problem to one of these helpful individuals. You will then be asked to wait outside. Your newly made contact will disappear inside the government office, re-emerging a little later to explain to you that your paperwork can be set right if you pay an additional fee in cash. You pay up. The paperwork gets sorted and you are on your way.

Exactly what happens inside the Immigration Office is not known to the authors.

Work permits

For small businesses involving a single foreign entrepreneur, after corporate arrangements have been established with your joint-venture partner, but before you can register your new business, you will need to obtain a work permit. The application for a work permit is filed at the Ministry of Labour if the company is located in Bangkok, or if located in the provinces, at the Department of Employment at the local City Hall.

The level of detail of documents to support a work permit application depends more on the nature of the business than its size. The difficulty of obtaining a work permit is related to two factors: whether a Thai could do the specified job, and the strength of the foreign applicant's qualification to do it. The fewer the skills of applicants, the less the government of Thailand considers it needs their services. It may be easier to get permission to build an oil refinery than to open what might be an expat's favourite business venture – a bar. As a result, thousands of foreigners in Thailand take their chances and work without permits.

There are minor exemptions to the need for permits in particular cases. Under some circumstances, foreigners admitted to the kingdom to do work of an "urgent and essential nature" are allowed to work without a permit for a limited period. In addition, those in the kingdom for a BOI-promoted project do need a work permit but are allowed to commence work while issuance of the permit is still pending.

But in most cases a work permit is required before starting the business.

An impressive dossier of information is needed to support a work permit application, including your job description, company address details, a map of the workplace, passport with Non-Immigrant B visa, proof of qualifications, CV plus letters of recommendation from former employers, a police clearance from your home country, a medical certificate from a Thai doctor testifying your general good health and freedom from specified diseases, photographs of the correct size and specified dress code, company incorporation documents and proof that the company being incorporated has applied for a tax ID and VAT registration. The normal time to issue a work permit is two to three weeks. If your application for a work permit contains even a minor blemish, the application will most likely be rejected, in which case the clock on the submission for a work permit restarts at zero and you have to start over.

The alternative to preparing documents yourself is to enlist the help of a lawyer. Assisting foreigners obtain work permits is a minor industry among the legal fraternity in Thailand. Though it will cost, engaging a lawyer who knows the ropes is certainly likely to be quicker and easier than tackling the Thai bureaucracy unaided.

Whether you hire a lawyer or not, the monthly fee payable on a work permit is 5,000 baht.

Rules regarding work permits reflect the government's policy of barring foreigners from employment that Thais can perform. Your work permit is valid only for the work it specifies. This rule is particularly irksome to many foreign owners in small businesses since it can be applied to the most trivial task such as wiping down a bar top, selling a customer a drink, or fixing a leaking tap. If you are judged by the authorities to be performing tasks outside those specified in the work permit, the law prescribes stern penalties – a mix of fines and/or jail terms and/or deportation.

Worse is working without a work permit at all. Despite that, many foreigners in Thailand work part-time or full-time jobs without work permits. But should the authorities choose to bring a prosecution, foreigners caught working without a work permit face an exacting mix of jail and fines (as prescribed by Section 51 of the Alien Working Act 2551 (2008)).

As a footnote to this section, we note that two different words are used in English translations of the Alien Working Act, the Foreign Business Act and other laws relating to rules of employment. These words are "alien" and "foreigner". In the context of business and employment laws, both words mean either a non-Thai individual, or a company (juristic person) that does not have the level of Thai ownership prescribed under Thai regulations.

Taxation

Thailand has tax treaties with 56 countries, a number that is likely to increase as governments across the world rationalise their cross-border tax affairs in an endeavour to curb tax evasion. (For the full list of countries, refer to www.rd.go.th/publish/766.0.html.)

A wide range of references are available detailing Thai tax rates. The PwC Thai Tax 2012 Booklet (all 102 pages) gives comprehensive details of tax rates and obligation at 31 March 2012 (full document at www.pwc.com/en_TH/th/tax/assets/2012/thai-tax-2012-booklet. pdf). The following is a summary of taxes on business in Thailand.

The accounting year
The accounting year in Thailand is the same as the calendar year, i.e. from 1 January until 31 December.

Income tax
Thailand has a marginal tax rate that increases with income. At the time of writing, the tax-free threshold income is 150,000 baht per annum, which means that the majority of people in Thailand probably won't be paying much income tax. From this threshold income, the tax rate increases in four steps to a maximum of 37%. Employers are responsible for deducting employees' taxes from their income monthly and remitting it to the tax office.

Capital Gains Tax (CGT)
Capital gains are taxed with income. Capital losses are not allowed as an offset in assessing capital gains. However, many capital gains are exempt from tax, including gains on share transactions.

Corporate Income Tax (CIT)
The corporate tax rate varies with profit on a sliding scale. CIT is self-assessed and must be paid every six months, from 1 January to 30 June and from 1 July to 31 December. Tax returns must be filed within 150 days of the due date.

Value-Added Tax (VAT)
Value-added tax is assessed similarly to VAT in most other countries on the difference between cost and sale price of goods/services being provided. The current rate of tax is 7%. Numerous exemptions apply, as detailed in the PwC booklet and other references. To claim the VAT on goods supplied, businesses must

register for VAT at the Revenue Department. Currently companies with an annual turnover of over 1,800,000 baht are obliged to register as an "operator" for VAT. Below that, registration is optional. Those in the system must file VAT returns no later than the 15th day of the following month.

Special Business Tax (SBT)

For certain industry sectors, such as financial services and insurance, in which assessment of VAT is difficult, SBT, an alternative tax to VAT is imposed. SBT is assessed at a percentage of gross revenue at a scale that varies between one industry and another. As with VAT, operators must file monthly tax returns no later than the 15th day of the following month.

House and Land Tax

Under the House and Land Tax Act of 1932, rentals on property attract a tax of 12.5% payable to the Revenue Department.

Other taxes

Various other business-related taxes, such as stamp duty and signboard tax, are also levied. These are detailed under their subject headings elsewhere in this book.

Business cards

In Thailand, exchanging name cards is the accepted form of passing on your name, contact details and occupation. Many people you meet in the course of an average day, and almost anyone you meet with even a remote chance of conducting some business with you, is likely to press a name card or a business card into your hand. Not doing so in a business setting would be considered impolite and unprofessional. As anywhere, business cards come in all shapes and sizes and colours.

The information printed on Thai business cards is pretty much typical of anywhere – name, address, occupation and qualifications (if any). We do suggest, however, that for Thailand the information is printed back and front, one side in English, the other in Thai. In

Thailand some people also incorporate a slightly up-market feature on their cards – a plastic coating to preserve them from the humid environment.

Some years ago in Asia, correct protocol for handling business cards was to hand out your card with both hands and receive an offered business card the same way. This cultural oddity seems to have died in recent years. Nevertheless in handing your card over, if you depart from the traditional two-handed pass, you should offer it in your right hand rather than the left. Another suggestion on the subject of business card handling (assuming you are at a desk or table) is to place the card on the table in front of you for a while, and perhaps comment on it, before placing it in your wallet, or wherever you store business cards.

Advertising

According to market survey company Nielsen, the total advertising spend by medium in Thailand for the first five months of 2013 was per the following table:

ADVERTISING EXPENDITURE

Medium	Baht (millions)	% of total	% change from previous year
TV	28,285	62.0	3.6
Newspaper	5,900	12.9	-3.2
Cinema	2,455	5.4	-17.7
Radio	2,451	5.4	0.0
Magazine	2,080	4.6	-2.6
Outdoor	1,711	3.8	-8.4
Transit	1,329	2.9	22.6
In Store	1,053	2.3	8.2
Internet	363	0.8	55.1
Total	45,627	100.0	

Source: Nielsen AdEx, 7 June 2013

It should be emphasised that these numbers record *spending* rather than effectiveness in selling the product. We have been unable to find any reliable figures on how spending on various types of advertising translates into sales. We do note, however, that from a low base, the fastest-rising advertising medium in recent years is the internet. Figures for mid-2013 showed that the internet was used by 52 million people in Thailand (77% of the population), thanks to the increasing use of smart phones and the extension of the broadband network. This was an increase of 45% over the previous year. These numbers might well understate the likely internet penetration into markets for consumer products, given that those without internet access are largely the rural poor who are unlikely to be buyers for anything other than the most basic goods.

Note: Signs outside business premises are subject to "Signboard Tax" at a rate calculated in baht per unit area. The rate of tax varies with the language on the sign, with signs written in English attracting over 13 times the rate charged for signs written in Thai! Further information can be found on the Mazars website (www.mazars.co.th/Home/Doing-Business-in-Thailand/Tax/Signboard-Tax-in-Thailand).

Banking

The baht

The currency of Thailand is the baht. The satang is the minor unit, at one-hundredth of a baht. Since the baht is a low-value currency, to most people the satang is of nuisance value only. Coinage covers currency denominations from 25 satang up to 10 baht, with notes of incremental value from 20 baht to 1,000 baht in circulation.

Bank of Thailand

Currency is issued by the Bank of Thailand (BOT), established in 1942 as the country's central bank. The role of the Bank is to act as banker to the government and other banks, represent the government in dealing with international monetary organisations and manage public debt. The Bank also acts as a lender of last resort for commercial banks by offering rediscount facilities for government securities, and negotiating short-term loans.

For the first few years after 1990, Thai business believed its own publicity that their country was one of the all-conquering Asian Tigers of the world economy. In the early nineties the economy roared along to seemingly effortless prosperity. Like in all the economic cycles that have repeated over history, economists were terribly surprised when the boom suddenly came to an end in the Asian Financial Crisis of 1997. Matters came to a head when the baht, which had to that time been loosely pegged to the US dollar, was attacked by Western currency traders, in particularly the legendary George Soros.

The Bank of Thailand spent a fortune of taxpayers' money to no avail trying to defend the baht. The Bank eventually admitted defeat, removing the dollar peg on 2 July 1997. By October 1997 the value of the baht had dropped by about 60% in relation to the US dollar to a record low of 55 baht to the dollar, before recovering.

Foreign exchange was difficult to obtain in Thailand at that time. Businesses which had borrowed in offshore currencies found their debt in baht increasing rapidly. At the stock exchange, the SET (Securities Exchange of Thailand) index slumped from 1,400 points in June 1996 to 200 points in June 1998. Banks came under pressure from loans collateralised by paper valuations of property and share assets that had plunged in value.

In 1998 the International Monetary Fund (IMF) arrived to officiate. The IMF rendered its standard economic prescription of privatising public corporations, raising taxes, reducing government spending and closing illiquid financial institutions.

In response, the Thai government treated the IMF to the same passive resistance that the Thai kings of the 19th century afforded quasi-Western institutions of the European colonisation period. Thailand accepted the IMF's US$17 billion assistance package, closed down selected financial institutions, raised the rate of VAT, but dragged its feet on privatising its most important assets. After the IMF departed the scene to fix the problems of the next ailing country, Thailand and its investors recovered their confidence. As a result, utilities which the IMF wanted privatised and sold to foreign interests, such as the electricity company EGAT, the Petroleum

Authority of Thailand (PTT), the Metropolitan Authority of Bangkok (MWA) and transport systems, remained in government hands.

As in the Global Financial Crisis (GFC) in the US and Europe a decade later, the Thai government in 1997 bailed out a number of the biggest banks on the same "too big to fail" principle. As in the GFC, the bailout package of the troubled banking industry was controversial. The bankers' critics held that the industry had caused its own problems through its imprudent lending practices, and were let off too easily at taxpayers' expense.

Thai bankers cleaned up their act after the 1997 financial crisis, suggesting that regulation of banking practices instigated by the IMF and implemented by the Thai government had most likely worked. In 2008, Thailand's banks made it through GFC relatively unscathed. No major banks went bankrupt this time around. No government bailouts were required.

Currently Thailand may be one of the safer countries of the world in which to do your banking ... at least for now. The history of finance suggests that regulating and deregulating the banking industry repeats on a multi-decadal cycle as bankers retire and a new crop of optimistic spirits is recruited to the industry.

Commercial banks

In 2014 there were 15 local commercial banking firms in Thailand with 2,700 branches, including head offices. Of these, 757 were in Bangkok and 1,943 in the provinces. In addition, there were 15 foreign banks in Thailand with at least one branch, and almost 30 overseas banks with offices in Thailand operating banking services but not fully established in the country. The commercial banking network reaches practically every town in the country. Despite the ready availability of banks, bank finance is difficult for foreigners to get. Joint ventures with majority Thai ownership may fare better depending on what collateral the Thai partners are prepared to offer. At time of writing, not all banks offer internet banking. One that does is Thailand's largest bank, the Bangkok Bank. Debit cards and ATM cards are readily available. Credit cards on Thai banks can be hard for foreigners to get.

Inward transfers

Foreigners holding a work permit may open Thai baht and foreign currency accounts with authorised banks in Thailand without limit. However, you will need to get Bank of Thailand approval for inward transfers of over US$20,000. While this is normally a formality, if required you can divide the amount you want to transfer into amounts under $20,000 that you can transfer as often as you want. For transfers over US$20,000, documents must be presented by the trading bank to the Bank of Thailand to verify that your source of funds is legitimate.

For inward transfers, you inform the sending bank of the name of the holder of the recipient account, recipient account number, the name, address and SWIFT code of the receiving bank in Thailand. We note that while the word SWIFT suggests the money will reach the destination bank without delay, this is not always the case. SWIFT is an acronym for *Society for Worldwide Interbank Financial Telecommunication*. Despite the electronic age, SWIFT transfers in our experience have sometimes taken as long as three weeks. Where the money spent its time between leaving the source bank account and arriving at its destination we were never able to establish!

Outbound transfers

To transfer money out of Thailand, you'll also need to provide the same account details as inward transfers except that transfers to Europe also require that the recipient's account number is preceded with the recipient bank's IBAN code. Depending on arrangements with your bank, limits apply to the individual amounts you can transfer. Generally, in our experience, you get a better exchange rate if funds are converted by the Thai sending bank. On other hand, most Thai banks will exchange baht to US dollars, but not necessarily into other currencies.

Paying suppliers

The most common method of paying creditors is either cash or via internet bank transfers. Payment by cheque is not widely practised in Thailand. Buying on credit is not universally popular either. Standing payments, such as for utilities, can be directly billed to and paid by banks.

Small change

Thailand is still very much a cash economy, with reasonably large sums being settled in bank notes, the largest denomination of which is the 1,000 baht note (about US$30 at current exchange rates). Credit cards are less widely accepted than in the West. This applies particularly in smaller towns in rural areas. But there is no need to carry wads of cash on your person since debit cards are usually accepted and ATMs are widespread and linked into international networks such as PLUS (Visa) or Cirrus (MasterCard). Since the exchange rates are based on the wholesale bank rate, ATM exchange rates are better than those at money changers, at least for small sums.

Investing in the stock exchange

The Securities Exchange of Thailand (SET) was established in 1974 under the supervision of the Ministry of Finance and the Bank of Thailand. To monitor and supervise the operations of the SET, the Office of the Securities and Exchange Commission (SEC) was set up in 1992. In the same year, to give new dimensions to the capital market, seven mutual fund management companies were licensed to give the general public a chance to participate in the investment through Unit Trusts.

Foreigners with a work permit are entitled to invest in the Thai stock exchange. Paperwork required includes copies of passport pages, copies of the work permit, copies of a bank statement for the previous six months, and "other (unspecified) related documents". Assuming the documentation is approved you then must lodge a minimum of 500,000 baht to secure an opening portfolio. Capital gains tax is not levied on profit of sale of SET-listed securities but dividends received from listed companies will be subject to withholding tax of 10%.

Made in Thailand

Twenty years ago, goods made in Thailand were generally perceived by Thais to be of inferior quality to those made in first-world countries. For high-end consumer goods, such as fancy cars, brand loyalty by country of origin remains as strong as ever. Customers for luxury Mercedes and BMW models continue to pay the 200% import duty for the pleasure of riding around in high-status vehicles. But with most of the world's major car companies now producing cars assembled in Thailand (including Mercedes and BMW low-end models), and for consumer products more generally, the perception of overseas superior quality has narrowed.

That said, Thais are as brand-conscious as their counterparts elsewhere in the world, and for many Thais, country of origin is still one of the most highly regarded criteria determining the perceived quality of the brand. Products from manufacturers from Japan, Korea, Taiwan, Germany and the United States are thought to be high-quality. Goods from the rest of Europe will rank not far behind. Goods from places like Africa, South America and Australia are not normally well known in the market place and may be overlooked if equivalent goods are available from the countries recognised as offering high-quality standards.

Luxury goods of respected brands on products such as fine wine, perfume and designer clothes are much valued in Thailand. Labels are important – a bag from a designer brand will be re used until it becomes shabby. Packaging is also important. Thais are artistic regarding possessions. A gift will generally be presented gift wrapped or inside an up-market bag.

As was the case for its role-model countries Japan and Korea, the Thai government has recognised the need to establish quality standards for locally made goods. Companies supplying auto and computer components from BOI's industrial parks will already be complying with the quality standards of their overseas partners. For broader industry, compliance with the ISO 9000 series of quality standards is common practice.

In addition to international standards, Thailand has its own national standards authority, Thailand Industrial Standard (TIS).

Most Thai standards are copies of US standards, translated into Thai. If you are obliged to comply with a TIS standard, your task will be simplified if you can find the overseas standard from which the TIS standard has been copied. One clue is to match the clause numbers of the TIS standard to its English-language equivalent. Another is to match technical words for which no equivalent word exists in Thai since general practice in writing the Thai standard is to adopt the same English word as the English language standard from which the Thai standard is created.

Chapter 6

Thai Society

Historical background

Thai society is a tightly structured hierarchy. At the top is the Buddhist order of monks. On the next level are the king and the royal family. Beneath that are two groups that hold most of the power and money in Thailand – the military and a moneyed elite, many of them Chinese, who manage much of the country's economy. A step further down the hierarchy are public servants and a growing middle class. At the bottom in terms of status but outnumbering all other levels combined are farmers and unskilled workers.

The present population of Thailand is about 67 million, about 75% of whom are descendants of the original settlers. Of the balance, 14% are Chinese, although intermarriage has blurred the distinction between Thais and Chinese. The other 11% are descendants of immigrants who entered the country over the years from India, Sri Lanka, and neighbours Myanmar, Cambodia and Vietnam – all countries with which Thailand has fought interminable wars over many centuries.

During the 19th century, a series of politically savvy Siamese kings, conscious of the threat of colonisation, nevertheless continued to trade with Europe and China without being subservient to either. King Rama V (1868–1910), better known as King Chulalongkorn, sent his children – of whom he had over a hundred from 73 partners – to schools in Russia, Germany, Britain and France where they could keep tabs on the European political scene.

While adopting some of the ways of the West, the 19th-century Siamese continued their divide-and-rule strategy to exploit rivalries between the competing colonial nations of Europe. The main threat in the region was France, which annexed countries to the east – Cambodia, Vietnam and Laos – and amalgamated them into French Indochina. Britain, in the midst of its "gunboat diplomacy" period, was the second most threatening colonial power, having colonised nearby Burma, Malaya and India. The king knew that Britain and France were traditional enemies. To keep the French at bay and the British on its side, Siam granted Britain most-favoured-nation status and preferential tax treatment for trade in and out of Siam.

In the 20th century, the country continued its policy of avoiding trouble from the rest of the world. The Thais joined in the First World War on the side of the Allies too late to participate in the conflict but in time to share the spoils of victory.

In 1932 the army staged a coup that removed the absolute power of the monarchy. Modern Thailand was proclaimed a democratic kingdom in 1939. Threatened by the Japanese, Thais sided with the Axis powers in WWII. The Japanese occupied Thailand between December 1941 and 1945 as a protective force without damaging the country too much. After the war concluded Thailand was quick to declare its allegiance to the winning side, convincing the US it would serve as a partner against the looming threat of communism.

Thailand's first election was held in 1946. From there to the present, a fragile democracy has ruled the country with frequent interludes of martial law while squabbling politicians sorted out their grievances. The army has staged 19 military coups since 1939, including the coup at time of writing, when martial law was declared on 20 May 2014.

For the most part, today's Thailand is a harmonious multiracial society. The major exception has its roots in the Anglo-Siamese Treaty of 1909 when Britain ceded the four southernmost provinces – Pattani, Narathiwat, Songkhla and Yala – from Malaya to Thailand. As was customary for European colonial affairs at the time, the views of the mainly Malay local population were ignored. Religious-inspired violence in the southern provinces continues to the present day. Since 2004, an estimated 6,000 people have been killed and 10,000 injured in conflicts between authorities and separatist Malay Muslims. The southernmost provinces are probably not the best places for foreigners to establish their businesses.

The monarchy

Buddhism in Thailand greatly influences behaviour in homes, social settings and in the business environment. But in terms of influencing day-to-day Thai behaviour, the monarchy runs Buddhism a close second. Visitors to Thailand can't help but notice that on public buildings, light standards, and billboards, poles, trees, towers and whatever structure will support signage are thousands of pictures of the Thai royal family, in particular the king, and tens of thousands of the king's and queen's personal flags (respectively yellow and blue). Portraits of the king and queen hang in every second office. In addition, bumper stickers, signs on *samlors*, T-shirts, etc, can carry a simple message, proclaim people's affection for the royal couple.

King Bhumibol Adulyadej, otherwise known as King Rama IX, came to the throne in 1946 after the death of his elder brother, Ananda Mahidol. Since then the king's personality and prestige have made him a pillar of political and social stability in a somewhat tumultuous political period.

At time of writing, the king is 86 years old and is frequently in and out of hospital dealing with various ailments. He is rarely seen in public. The community worries about his likely successor. None of the candidates has anything like the king's profile and respect. Political uncertainty from an imminent change to the monarchy may be a consideration for those evaluating whether to establish business in Thailand.

On the subject of royalty, it is worth noting that Thailand has strict lèse-majesté laws to prohibit people criticising the royals.

Penalties for those falling foul of these laws have been severe. Foreigners in Thailand are advised to avoid discussing the Thai royals while in the kingdom. Foreigners are also advised to stay neutral if the subject of politics comes up during a conversation with Thais – at least until you've determined the politics of your conversation partner!

Shaping young minds

The underlying cultural unit in Thailand is the extended family, in which every member has a prescribed role. The father is regarded as the leader of the household, but the mother conducts most of the day-to-day management of family affairs. Children, uncles, aunts, grandparents and the wider community – all have their own niches in the hierarchy. As they grow up, children are assigned certain household duties according to age and ability. A prime responsibility that children learn at a young age is their duty of care to their parents in later life. The elderly have an honoured place in the household.

Notions of hierarchy are reflected in the complex vocabulary the Thai language has developed for family members. Not only are there words for mother, father, siblings, uncles, aunts and cousins, Thai has specific words for father's father (*pu*), mother's father (*ya*), mother's father (*ta*), mother's mother (*yai*), older brother (*pi chai*), younger brother (*nong chai*), older sister (*pi sao*) and younger sister (*nong sao*). Peripheral to the immediate family is the extended family of close relatives, distant relatives, friends or even mistresses who are referred to as aunts, uncles and cousins according to their age and gender, and afforded the deference appropriate to their classifications.

One of the visible signs of social standing is the *wai*, the traditional Thai greeting and acknowledgment. Thai mothers teach their children to wai from infanthood, delivering different wais in accordance with the status of each member of the family receiving the wai. Young children schooled in the protocols of delivering and receiving wais will get to know who's boss around the house before they learn to speak.

School days and beyond

The Thai education system comprises four levels: one or two years of pre-school, six years of compulsory primary education, six years of secondary education, followed by higher education. Class sizes are large (between 30 and 50 students).

The first culture shock for Thai children comes early when they first meet their pre-school teacher (*a-charn*), upon whom, they learn, has been conferred the status of a minor god, and who must be treated accordingly. The traditional view of Thai education is that students in Thai schools are afforded the status of naughty boys who are meant to be seen, but not heard. Teachers are considered to be all-knowing. Questioning the teacher borders on impertinence. Students are taught by rote. Critical thinking is not encouraged.

The dictatorial nature of Thai teaching practice has been criticised by Western experts in education as producing incurious adults conditioned to obey rather than to question. Years of deference to teachers are thought to reinforce a sense of hierarchy and authority that children might have already acquired from their earliest days. Those who move from secondary school to the workplace may carry with them notions that their status in their new career – and more generally their prospects in life – are preordained.

Religious attitudes

Buddhism arrived in Siam from India perhaps as early as 2,000 years ago. Buddhism comes in three main forms – the Mahayana, the Theravada, and the Mendicant. Thailand has adopted the Theravada variant of Buddhism, as have the neighbouring countries of Cambodia, Laos and Myanmar.

Other religions in Thailand have smaller followings. Muslim missionaries arrived in Thailand with Arab traders from the 16th century onwards and Christian missionaries arrived from the 17th century. Both Islamic and Christian missionaries tried to convert Thai kings to their respective faiths without success. In displays of passive resistance that have served Thailand well over the centuries, missionaries were allowed to practise their faiths but none of the kings converted from Buddhism. Christian missionaries were no more successful at converting the wider population. In fact the reverse has occurred, with the current king regarded as nominal head of all religions in the country, including Christianity!

About 95% of Thais are Buddhist and most engage with their religion on a daily basis, waiing to monks, lighting incense sticks at temples and gaining merit by contributing to the food bowls of monks. About 3% of the population of Thailand is Muslim, mostly people from the southern provinces bordering Malaysia. The remaining 2% are of other religions such as Christianity, or declare themselves to be non-religious. As evidence that the religion is alive and well, there are over 40,000 Buddhist temples in Thailand, with dozens more under construction.

Since Buddhism is the prevailing religion, most of the Thai staff you are likely to hire for your business will be Buddhists. The complexities of Buddhist beliefs are beyond the scope of this book. But some of the keys ideas of Theravada Buddhism are of self-improvement, social tranquillity and placid acceptance of the trials and tribulations of life.

Buddhism is a highly personal religion with no strong ideology or dogma and little structured religious worship. It imposes almost no requirements on the visitor or non-believer other than a reasonable code of behaviour and dress when interacting with monks and entering religious shrines, such as temples.

Buddhism is more pervasive in everyday life than Christianity, which preoccupies most of its adherents only for an hour or two a week. Nevertheless Buddhism has no compulsion to proselytise. Religious beliefs of others are of little concern to Buddhists. No Buddhist Crusades have been mounted to teach the infidels a thing or two. Nor has a Buddhist Inquisition burned heretics at the stake.

Even so Buddhists are not always at peace with themselves and others. Nor are monks, clad only in an orange shroud, necessarily as bereft of possessions as they appear. There have been occasional outbreaks of violence by Thai Buddhists against Muslims – and even against tourists. With the ostensible purpose of funding temple extensions or erecting larger Buddha statutes than the temple down the street, temples customarily indulge in money-making activities. Abbots who have accumulated great wealth are not entirely unheard of.

One of the main teachings in Buddhism is belief in rebirth, whereby every life, be it human or animal, is only a phase in a cycle of innumerable lives, and every good or bad deed incurs an appropriate consequence in some future life. Buddhism also teaches that to attain happiness one must follow the "Middle Path", that is, the path between the two extremes of over-indulgence and rigorous self-discipline. In pursuing the middle path, believers practise self-control and avoid conflict in day-to-day dealings with others.

Belief in karma, controlled demeanour and a fatalistic mindset have important implications in the workplace. Avoiding conflict is but a step away from failure to express a contrary opinion, in particular to someone in authority. Such an attitude is contrary to Western practice where underlings may experience sheer delight in explaining to the boss that he/she is getting it wrong, By contrast, a Thai might realise the boss is about to make a monumental blunder, but may elect to keep quiet about it.

Blessing the workplace

In Thailand, as in most of Asia, business culture and etiquette is subtle. Thais are generous in making allowances for foreigners who don't quite keep abreast of local cultural nuances. However, complying with local customs will please the locals and raise their esteem of you.

Apart from its influence on the attitudes, behaviour and performance of employees, Buddhism requires tangible activities in the workplace. Among these are blessings and other ceremonies to be observed - and perhaps organised - by the employer.

When a company opens in Thailand, standard practice is for monks to bless the new premises. Thais believe that the blessing ceremony is a factor in determining whether a business will be successful or not. If you are the foreign manager or business owner, you may or may not agree with your staff on that point.

But if you authorise the opening ceremony, whatever problems your company experiences down the track won't be blamed on your failure to have the premises blessed in the approved manner.

Buddhist monks are happy to perform the ceremony in return for a modest donation to their temple. The first step is for the abbot to determine an auspicious day based on his astrological calculations. That done, on the day of the ceremony, organisers must transport the monks to and from the business. A minibus will suffice for this purpose. Normally six to nine monks will attend. A room large enough to accommodate the monks and the other participants must be provided. Seating details are important. Protocol dictates that the monks must be higher than anyone else, in accordance with their status in society. This requires a raised platform long enough for the monks to sit side by side facing the staff, who, to maintain the correct elevation difference between monks and those of lesser rank, would normally be sitting on the floor. Monks are adept at adopting the lotus position and do not normally require chairs. But since some senior monks are old men, it's worth checking this aspect in advance.

In preparation for the monks' arrival, consider having a staff member coach you in advanced waiing techniques, since if you are the company head, you will be the first in line to wai the monks when they arrive.

The ceremony itself may take an hour and is conducted entirely by the monks and requires little input from the attendees. The order of service is chanting in Pali, which most attendees won't understand, interspersed with prayers, also in Pali. Towards the end of the ceremony, members of staff as directed by monks and the monks themselves tie holy ribbons around convenient objects and post good-luck charms at strategic points around the building and may sprinkle holy water around to seal the deal with whatever spirits are looking down.

Since monks are forbidden to eat after midday, the completion of religious activities should be scheduled for around 11am. After the ceremony, a traditional feast of light meats, vegetables and fruits follows. Thais are familiar with the rules for handing food to monks, since their community provides this service daily. For the business blessing ceremony, the head of the client organization has the honour of serving the food first, with the highest-ranking monk being first served. If you, a foreigner, happen to be the head person, this may mean that a non-Thai is serving the monks directly. So prior to the event, get some advice on the minutiae of serving protocol.

Women should take special care, since women are not merely prohibited from touching a monk, they are also prohibited from touching any extension of the monk, including a food bowl or plate the monk might be holding. That women serve food to monks is commonplace, since every morning, monks head into the community seeking their breakfasts, of which at least half are likely to be served by women. A woman has three options when serving a monk his meal. She can drop the food into the monk's extended bowl, taking care to make no contact with the bowl or the monk himself. Or, instead of handing food directly to the monk, she can place the plate of food in front of the monk, perhaps on a handkerchief sized piece of cloth. Or she can hand the food over to a male associate to give to the monk. These protocols are in accordance with the monk's vow of celibacy and shouldn't be regarded as looking down on women. However, at the blessing ceremony, where the monk is likely to be sitting not standing, food is more likely to be served on a plate placed before the monk. If so, serving protocols by women are less complicated.

The monks get to eat first, and leave before noon. The ceremony then changes into a less structured social event. Organisers will lay on much more food than the monks are likely to eat, so that ample leftovers are available for the staff to enjoy after the monks have departed the scene.

Religious icons

Apart from the blessing ceremony, a certain amount of daily spiritual upkeep is advised at your business premises. In particular it will pay to investigate whether a spirit house should be provided to accommodate spirits inconvenienced by structures erected to serve your project. Since spirits are small in stature, they don't need a lot of space. A doll's-house-sized shelter mounted on a post is the accepted arrangement. Ideally the spirit house is located outside the premises in a position beyond the building's shadow – though spirit houses and altars inside premises are common enough. Readymade spirit houses can be bought at specialist roadside suppliers but before installation expert advice should be sought on their proposed site. Those not in the know can easily locate spiritual objects in inappropriate locations, in which case negative consequences for the business may ensue.

The spirit house is a convenient place for your staff to discharge prayers, make offerings of food, drape garlands of flowers, burn incense and generally make merit. Our observation is that the spirits themselves don't seem to take advantage of these offerings, which must be replaced from time to time before they rot. Usually those of your staff who wai the spirit house on arriving at work each day will refresh the food on offer as required and install new incense sticks and flowers.

The Chinese

Artisans and traders from China settled in Siam thousands of years ago. But the majority of Thailand's immigrant Chinese entered the country as labourers in the 19th century, during which the Chinese population in Thailand rose by over 300%. This itinerant Chinese labour, the majority single males, came to Siam to escape conflict in Southern China.

Somewhere around the mid-1850s, capitalism started to find its niche in Siam, but the majority of Thai people at the time were working in agriculture or for the state. They were not disposed to work in the factories in which the Chinese found jobs.

Chinese immigrants also supplied manual labour to construction projects in Bangkok, which was developing quickly at the time. After settling down in Thailand, the Chinese intermarried with the Siamese and moved into their more traditional activities in retail, commerce and banking. It is generally agreed that the Chinese in Thailand now wield disproportionate influence over the private sector, owning at least 50% of investment in the banking and finance sector, and 90% of investment in the manufacturing and commercial sectors.

The estimate that 14% of the population are Chinese is an approximate figure at best because the Chinese have now fully assimilated into Thai society. Few Thais can be sure they have no Chinese blood and the reverse applies.

Chinese traditions

From time to time the Chinese have been persecuted in Thailand, in particular during the 1930s after the military coup that toppled the monarchy. But since then harmony has reigned as the Chinese have increasingly lost their separate identity. Generally the Thai-Chinese subscribe fully to mainstream Thai values. Most of them, particularly those of the third generation or so, consider themselves very much "Thai". They speak Thai, eat Thai food, and struggle to obtain an education in the best Thai universities.

Though the Chinese assimilated into and intermarried with Thais generations ago, they like to preserve reminders of their background. For example many Thai-Chinese maintain Chinese religions and traditions in parallel with Thai religions and traditions. Alongside Buddha statues, your Thai-Chinese staff may have in their homes figures of Chinese gods and portraits of ancestors. Unlike Christianity and Islam, Buddhism does not require religious exclusivity. Buddhists can simultaneously subscribe to other faiths without feeling they have abandoned the Buddhist cause.

Thai-Chinese religious beliefs add further layers to those of Buddhism and animism and may also require an additional altar or two featuring various miniature figures of people, gods and animals. As for Buddhism, these altars may also require incense sticks and offerings of flowers, food and drink. Your staff will victual the altars of Chinese gods as required. The business proprietor merely needs to provide the space to accommodate what altars are required.

Chinese celebrate the Chinese New Year (around late January, early February) to pay respects to senior members of their families.

Shortly after they have retired their reindeer and Santa hats from Christmas of the previous year, Thai department stores will deck themselves out in red and gold and string up their Chinese lanterns to take advantage of another commercial opportunity.

Feng shui

Important to Thais and your business prospects are the *feng shui* aspects of any structures you might decide to build. Feng shui is an ancient belief system developed over 3,000 years ago in China. Whether you believe feng shui principles or not, other people may do so, as certain shopping centre proprietors in Bangkok have found out to their cost. If word spreads that your enterprise has bad feng shui, customers won't go there and feng shui will then become a self-fulfilling prophecy.

The term feng shui comes from the Chinese words *feng* ("wind") and *shui* ("water"), which in ancient China were related to good health. Feng shui principles, should you wish to acquire them, can be studied in great depth from readings and books widely available on the subject. Feng shui talks about the interaction of five elements – wood, fire, earth metal and water – and of energy fields generated by objects and features of buildings such as clocks, mirrors and fountains. The orientation of building features such as doors, windows, corridors and rooms is another important consideration as are colour combinations, pictures, wall hangings and water features such a fountains and aquariums.

Becoming a feng shui expert is no mean task. Should you wish to take the easy path and avoid the years of study required to equip yourself with the necessary feng shui expertise that will keep you and your business out of trouble, Thai-Chinese feng shui consultants who can advise you in the subject for a fee are readily available.

Unexpected spiritual influences

Even after blessing the premises, erecting shrines inside and spirit houses outside the building, hiring a feng shui advisor and taking his advice to paint your building a luminous green, if unexpected problems occur, you may find you have offended the spirits in some way that is bringing bad luck to your business.

Long-held superstitions die hard in Thailand.

Until recently, many Thai hairdressers closed on Wednesdays because of a Brahman belief that it is bad luck to cut hair on that particular day of the week.

When the Thai finance minister resigned in June 1997 during tough economic times, some parliamentarians suggested that the two large wooden elephant statues standing at the doors of the Finance Ministry were cursed and had jinxed him.

In 1956 the government embarked on a project to build the Erawan Hotel in Bangkok. Construction was plagued by a seemingly endless series of accidents, cost overruns and loss of materials. Suspicion first centred on the spirits of criminals who had once been put on public display nearby. But an astrologer determined that the real problem was the foundations of the building had been laid on the incorrect date. On the astrologer's recommendation, a shrine was built on the site to relieve this bad karma. After this, the hotel project proceeded without further incident.

So even if your life is driven by values stemming entirely from this earthly life, the same may not be true for your staff and other stakeholders in your business. Even armed with the best of all business plans, what enterprising foreign businessperson would realise such forces could be at work? Consulting spiritual advisors at an early stage of your project may not merely be good advice; it could also be good business.

Chapter 7

Stakeholders in the Business

Demographics

Thailand has experienced a massive change in its demographics in the last two generations. In the half decade from 1950 to 55, the total fertility rate (average number of children per mother) was 6.4. By 2013 this had dropped to 1.56. (To replace itself in the long term, a population needs to have a total fertility rate of 2.06 or above.) In the year 2000, 24.8% of the Thai population was aged 0–14 and 9.4% over 60. By 2030, demographers expect these ratios will have changed to 13.5% and 25% respectively (see *Thailand in Figures*). Thailand's population is projected to peak in 2025 at about 70.5 million, then gradually decline. Assuming that Thailand maintains its retirement age of 60 years, the percentage of the population available to the workforce will decline from 66% in 2000 to 61.4% in 2030.

These demographics may have a number of effects on long-term prospects for business in Thailand. One of the likely effects will be a shift from industries marketing youth-oriented products such as education to those required by older age groups, such as health care. Also the structure of the workforce will change: on average the workforce will be older and more experienced. And over a fairly long term, as the population declines and fewer people are entering than leaving it, the size of the workforce will diminish.

In this context, we should note that there is no old age pension in Thailand. Seventy-five percent of retirement-age people live with family or continue to work. Only a minority have sufficient savings to support themselves. With their dependencies taken care of by support groups, Thais past retirement age are unlikely to be a big spending group.

We note that a similar dramatic change of population profile has occurred in most of Thailand's Asian trading partners (as well as half the countries of Europe) – in 2012, the total fertility rate in Singapore was 1.2, South Korea's was 1.24, and China's was 1.56.

General labour statistics

In 2009, the population of Thailand was 67 million, of whom 37.5 million were in the country's workforce. At time of writing, Thailand's official unemployment is 0.7%, a rate of employment that would be the envy of many Western countries.

Below is a selection of statistics published by the International Labour Office, offering a brief profile of current labour conditions:

- Since 1997, wages growth has not kept pace with productivity growth.
- About 65% of labour is employed in the "informal" economy – defined as self-employed or employed in a family business.
- 50% of the workforce only has elementary or sub-elementary education (down from 65% in 2001, but still not high compared to other countries in the region).
- Average hours worked per week was 45.3.
- The gap in average monthly pay between men and women has decreased from 660 baht (in 2001) to 319 baht (in 2010).

Labour availability

Sometime during the first decade of the 21st century, the number of employees in the service sector of the Thai economy passed the number in agriculture for the first time. In 2010, 45.8% of the working population was engaged in the service sector (including government), while 40.7% were in agriculture. The balance of about 14% were occupied in manufacturing.

As noted above, in 2012 the economy was effectively in full employment. In addition to official figures there were an estimated three million migrant workers in Thailand, mostly from bordering countries – Myanmar, Laos and Cambodia – about two-thirds of them "irregular", meaning their presence in Thailand was illegal for one reason or another. Any employer who taps into this particular labour force takes the risk of an unfriendly visit from the Immigration Department. Since it's not possible from appearances to determine who's illegal and who isn't, foreigners starting up new businesses in Thailand are advised to check out the employment credentials of all prospective staff.

Thailand has no government-run employment or unemployment office from which staff can be recruited from the ranks of the unemployed. Rather the country operates largely on networking. By far the most common method of recruiting staff is by word of mouth – such as family members and extended family members recommending one another. Failing that, a range of private agencies supplying specific trades and skills can be consulted from internet websites.

Some Thai/foreign joint venturers prefer to recruit staff straight out of centres of learning rather than choosing older and more experienced people who have acquired passive attitudes working in offices of Thai companies. Those who wish to recruit newly qualified tertiary graduates can circulate their requirements to student placement departments of universities. Likewise those wishing to hire qualified tradespeople can hire from trade associations, most of which conduct outplacement operations. For example, for qualified welders you might consult PAE Thailand (www.pae.co.th/04-welder-certifications-center.php). Similar institutions exist for other trades.

Assembling a workforce

Depending on the business's size, those setting up in Thailand may bring some key people with them from their home office. But whatever the size of the business it is almost certain to require some local manpower. This section addresses the availability of suitable talent within Thailand, how staff might be recruited, expected levels of pay, cultural considerations in dealing with the workforce, how the expat manager relates to staff and superiors, and details of Thai labour laws.

Acts of Parliament relating to labour

About a dozen acts of parliament relate to the employment of labour in Thailand. English translations of these acts can be downloaded from the internet. Of these we consider the following worth consulting:

- Labour Protections Act 2541
- Labour Relations Act 2518
- Alien Working Act 2551
- Workers Compensation Act 2537

The English translations of the Acts are reasonably easy to read and understand, at least by the standards of your average legal document. Foreign entrepreneurs who want to investigate employee/ employer rights and entitlements can download the Acts for themselves. Alternatively they can consult a lawyer who will provide similar information for a fee.

We suggest you do both. Numerous aspects of the Acts are open to interpretation. Reading them in advance of seeing your lawyer will provide a basis for discussion. In addition, rules in relation to labour, like rules elsewhere, are constantly being modified. The rate of change of Thai law will most likely increase further when the AEC comes into force in 2015 and rewrites the rulebook. A competent lawyer should keep you up to date with your current obligations to the labour force.

The principal act concerning the hiring and firing of labour is the Labour Protection Act 2451. The following is a non-exhaustive list of some of the main obligations the Labour Protection Act imposes on employers:

- An employer employing subcontractors is responsible for paying wages due from subcontractors in the event the sub-contractor defaults on his staff payments (Section 12).
- If you buy a business as a going concern and in doing so maintain employment of existing staff you are obliged to pay any accrued staff benefits incurred by the previous owner (Section 13).
- Working hours at normal rate of pay is not to exceed 48 hours per week except for certain hazardous occupations when the maximum is 42 hours (Section 23).
- Overtime rate is one and a half times basic rate (Section 61).
- Working prescribed public holidays (see the list at the back of the book) attracts pay at twice the basic rate (Section 62) and overtime at twice the normal overtime rate – i.e. three times the basic rate (Section 63).
- With quite a large number of exceptions, for example tour-ist-related industries (Section 65), employees cannot be com-pelled to work public holidays
- If they do work holidays, they can either get a day off in lieu or get paid at holiday rates (Section 29).
- Annual paid holiday entitlement is six days (Section 30).
- Employees are entitled to paid sick leave for up to 30 days per annum. If sick leave extends longer than two days for a particular malady a medical certificate is required (Section 32).
- If male employees are required for military service, the employer is obliged to pay wages for the time taken off up to a maximum of 60 days per annum (Sections 35 and 58).
- A pregnant employee is entitled to a maximum 45 days of paid leave from the employer for each pregnancy (Section 41). Another 45 days' pay is collectable from the gov-ernment-run Social Welfare Fund to which the employer is obliged to subscribe.
- Minimum age for employees is 15 (Section 44).
- If an employer elects to cease operations and no alterna-tive work is available, the employer has to pay employees at

half the basic rate while employees are still employed even if there is no work for them to do.

- An employer who employs ten or more staff shall display in a conspicuous place work rules of the enterprise written in the Thai language (Section 108) and likewise records of personal details and pay of all employees shall be available at the workplace for viewing by the labour inspector from the Ministry of Labour.
- Severance pay at the basic rate for employees terminated not for cause (Section 119) is calculated on length of service as follows:
  - 120 days to a year of service – not less than 30 days' pay
  - One year to three years – not less than 90 days' pay
  - Three years to six years – not less than 180 days' pay
  - Six years to ten years – not less than 240 days' pay
  - More than ten years – not less than 300 days' pay
- This obligation is also imposed on employers who are going out of business for any reason (Section 118) or are moving their business to another location (Section 120).
- Employers with more than ten staff are obliged to contribute equally to an Employee Welfare Fund of which the employee is the beneficiary. The law relating to this fund is covered under a separate act, the Provident Fund Act 1987. The amount contributed by each party to this fund will not be less than 3% and no greater than 15% of gross pay (Section 6 of the Provident Fund Act).

Hiring and firing

Because they tend to develop tight social groups at work, firing poorly performing employees in Thailand may damage office morale to a greater degree than in the West. This is one of the reasons downsizing is uncommon in Thailand. Rather than being told to leave, employees who fail to cut the mustard in Thai companies tend to be moved sideways. Another strategy is to give non-performing employees a job they dislike in the hope they will leave of their own accord.

As noted above, the formula for calculating severance pay for employees terminated not for cause is detailed in Section 118 of the Labour Protection Act of 1999. Employers are exempted from this requirement if the employee is being fired for offences committed by the employee against the employer as defined in Section 119 of the Labour Protection Act. Since it is a whole lot more difficult to fire employees than hire them, it is worth thoroughly checking references and qualifications before offering anyone a job.

Employees' military and religious obligations
Young male employees may go absent from their workplace for two reasons other than sickness and study leave.

Every year the military in Thailand determines the level of manpower they need for the following 12 months of operations. If sufficient volunteers are attracted to the service to fill the quota, nothing else happens. If not, the military conscripts the balance of its recruits from males who have turned 21 in that particular year. Recruitment Day for national service is in the first week of April. On that day, all males aged 21 who don't have an exemption are obliged to attend their registered place of birth to participate in a lottery. On their return to their village, the unwilling participants gather at a meeting hosted by the military. Those eligible for the draft are called to a stage one at a time and told to draw a card out of a canister. If they draw a red card, the military has them for two years. If they draw a black card, they return to civilian life.

In addition to military service, some young male Buddhists also feel an obligation to be ordained as part-time monks. Temporary ordination is usually conducted over the summer months – from June to October. During that time the candidate will be absent from work, living at the local temple complex, where he will participate in the same rituals as his more senior fellows. There is no fixed duration for a temporary ordination. Twenty-four hours would be brief; one to three months more likely. As with employees on military service, under the Labour Protection Act employers must continue to pay employees undergoing ordination for a maximum of 60 days as prescribed by Sections 35 and 58 of the act.

Rates of pay

Each of Thailand's 76 provinces sets its own minimum pay rate. In 2012 the minimum wage for Bangkok and six other provinces was set at 300 baht per day. This is about 9,000 baht a month for the normal six-day week widely worked in Thailand. If you look at page 8 of *Costs of Doing Business in Thailand* (www.boi.go.th), you will note this is pretty much the monthly pay for semi-skilled workers, drivers, typists, and office clerical workers. It's not a lot less than you would pay for an accountant! Average figures for other occupations are as listed in the booklet. It should be noted there are wide regional variations for pay rates in Thailand, with Bangkok and tourist areas being highest and border areas with Cambodia and Laos the lowest.

Labour unions

Thailand is not a strongly unionised country. Having been brought up from birth with the idea that an individual's spot in life's hierarchy has to a great extent been predetermined, Thais are not culturally inclined to align with unionism's traditional preoccupations of better pay and conditions. More than most places, underprivileged Thais tend to accept the status quo. Less than 4% of the private sector workforce of around nine million people (1% of the total workforce) belong to a union.

Nevertheless, the 2007 constitution guarantees freedom of association for unions and for the population more generally. As has been apparent from political street demonstrations in recent times, this right has been upheld. On the other hand, labour unions are restricted by divide-and-rule provisions in legislation that prevent disputes from widening beyond an individual firm. Other restrictive covenants also apply.

The Labour Relations Act of 1975 is Thailand's principal law covering rights between employers and private employees. Some key points of the legislation are:

- Only one union is permitted per enterprise (no unions are permitted for specific trades).

- Loss of employment with an enterprise also means loss of union membership (this follows from previous rule).
- A union can be dissolved if its membership falls below 25% of the eligible workforce.
- The Ministry of Labour must approve whatever advisors that unions wish to employ.
- Civil servants and those providing "essential services" do not have the right to join unions.
- Companies employing 20 or more employees are obliged to write an agreement specifying pay and conditions.
- If a dispute cannot be resolved between employees and employer it is referred to a "conciliation officer" appointed by the government and is heard by a government-appointed arbiter.

Labour unions are present in fewer than half of Thailand's provinces and are considered ineffective in BOI's industrial estates, where they otherwise might be thought to be most active.

Workers Compensation Act 2537

Under the Workers Compensation Act of 2537, employers must register for Workers Compensation with the Ministry of Labour and Social Welfare. For employees injured or killed as a result of accidents at work, they or their dependants (in the event of fatal accidents) are entitled to compensation for medical, rehabilitation or funeral costs. If employees fail to return to work after an accident, 60% of wages is payable for the following time periods after the loss-of-time accident (Section 18):

- For an accident involving no loss of organs – up to 1 year
- For an accident involving loss of organs – up to 10 years
- For an accident involving disablement – up to 15 years
- For an accident resulting in death – up to 8 years

In addition, employers must pay contributions of up to 5% of wages into a Workers Compensation Fund operated by the Ministry of

Labour and Social Welfare which adjudicates on disputes, if any, between employers and employees.

Occupational Safety, Health and Environment Act

Section 8 of the Occupational Health and Safety Act 2554 states: "An Employer is required to administer, manage, and operate the occupational safety, health and environment in conformity with the standards prescribed in the Ministerial Regulation" (www.labour.go.th/en/).

The act requires the employer to appoint a qualified safety officer plus staff approved by the Department of Labour Protection and Welfare (Section 13) and to provide safety training to employees (Section 16).

From observation, activities at factories and building sites suggest that safety practices prescribed by the act, at least in the small-business sector, have not been widely adopted. According to 2009 employment statistics, only 9.3 million of the 37 million workforce were insured under the social security system. In dimly lit factories, workers operate machines without guards, building sites are without the normal safety accessories of the West – adequate scaffolding, hard hats and safety shoes. We think it doubtful that many small-business operators are appointing safety officers and filing safety plans in accordance with the provisions of act.

However, that the act exists should be borne in mind.

Alien Working Act

One of the restrictions most likely to displease foreign small-business entrepreneurs in Thailand is embodied in the Alien Working Act 2551. To do any work at all in your business, you, as a foreign entrepreneur, need a work permit that will, with the exception of unusual circumstances like national emergencies, only be granted if the job description is for a job that a Thai can't readily do. For example if your business is retail, your job description as marketing manager does not entitle you to take money for a sale. Likewise if you are a bar owner you cannot legally wash a glass or prepare a set of accounts. These are jobs a Thai can readily do.

Some foreign small-business proprietors ignore the rules and risk incurring the mix of heinous penalties the act prescribes for their transgressions. Others may spend their days perched on a stool surveying their domain. To tourists, the more law-abiding foreign bar owners may look perpetually lazy. In truth they may merely be performing job descriptions defined by their work permits – perhaps as marketing managers sharing a drink with their customers, perhaps as personnel managers closely supervising their staff.

Who enforces the law?

The laws as written suggest a small army of government inspectors roaming the commercial world, enforcing its various laws. The Alien Working Act defines a "Competent Official" appointed by the Minister of Labour as the enforcer of its law. The Workers Compensation Act also appoints a "Competent Official" as the agent of enforcement. The Labour Protection Act assigns enforcing duties to a "Labour Inspector", the Labour Relations Act to a "Conciliation Officer" and the Occupational Safety and Environment Act, to a "Safety Officer".

If your business is large, you may conceivably get a visit from any of these card-carrying officials. But from our experience, if you are running a small business, if anyone turns up at your workplace to question your labour practices, it's most likely to be a local policeman whose rights under the various acts are uncertain, whose actions are unpredictable, but who acts as if he is empowered with unlimited authority.

As a general rule, the police don't advertise their intended visits in advance. They just arrive. The ever-present threat of an untimely visit from the law is stressful for many small-business operators since there are so many regulations which police can accuse you of violating. Unless you sit in a chair at your business-place doing absolutely nothing, have all your records in order, or have established a friendly relationship with your local policemen, ever present in the back of your mind is that someone may have seen you performing an illegal act like moving a box or adjusting a chair.

If you *have* stepped over the line, or the police suggest you have, you face a mix of stern penalties – fines, jail and deportation. This risk, plus the associated boredom of doing next to nothing one day after the next, is an aspect that prospective small-business entrepreneurs should bear in mind in evaluating their options before taking the plunge into a small business in Thailand.

Contact with authorities

Harassment of foreigners suspected of not having correct business licences is common. This is particularly the case for frivolous industries in which the government might like to discourage foreign participation, but falls short of banning it. The accepted method of dealing with police in foreign/Thai joint ventures is to get the Thai partner to take care of matters. Thais are more adept in establishing and providing whatever incentives the police require for leaving you alone.

Apart from their activities enforcing Acts of Parliament at the business premises of foreigners, police in Thailand do all the things they usually do in most countries. Their most visually evident activity is directing and monitoring traffic. Police checks at road blocks are prevalent on major roads. Such is the importance of the tourist industry to Thailand that police are under instruction not to hassle tourists unnecessarily. Mostly you get waved through once you wind down your car window and police have determined you are not a Thai. Some ask where you are going, or where you came from. Sometimes they do a licence check.

On the question of driving entitlements in Thailand, in order of preference, the most valid licence for driving a car in Thailand is a Thai licence, followed by an international licence followed by a licence from your home country.

For motorbikes, the rules are similar. A car driving licence does not cover driving a bike.

Anyone taking up residence in Thailand and intending to drive is advised to obtain a Thai licence as soon as possible. A licence will normally be issued in one day subject to your passing a test of Thai driving laws, a colour blindness test and a test of your reflexes.

The documents you need to bring to the driving test centre are a copy of your home country or international licence (if you have one), a medical certificate testifying that you are fit to drive, and evidence of your address (a copy of a utilities bill at a minimum but a letter from immigration is more acceptable). Doctors in Thailand know which medical form to fill out to support the licence application. The fee for licence issue is only 100 baht, but all in you will need about 1,000 baht to cover the licence itself, the health certificate, the proof of address from immigration, and photography. Photos embedded in the licence are taken on the spot as part of the licence issue. Your initial licence is for a year. After getting through this probationary period without mishap, the licence period is extended for five years.

Apart from its convenience when driving, a driving licence as a form of ID is a handy alternative to a passport for expats living in Thailand, where a number of commercial institutions, or even gatekeepers at gated communities, will ask you to lodge ID before allowing you to enter their premises. Theoretically as a foreigner in Thailand you are meant to carry a passport on your person everywhere you go. Very few foreigners do so, though some do tuck a copy of their passport photo page into their wallets or handbags.

But a driving licence is almost always acceptable as ID. A driving licence which fits into your wallet or your purse is far more convenient and contains more personal information than your passport since it not only includes your photo, your name and your passport number but also your home address in Thailand. And if the worst comes to the worst, loss of a driving licence will involve you in far less hassle than loss of a passport (along with all the visa stamps, entry and exit permits, etc that entitle you to stay in the country).

Vehicles you are driving, whether hired, leased or owned, need to be insured with road tax paid in advance. Various statistics attest that traffic accidents are distinctly more likely in Thailand than most places. Thais seem to lose their easygoing personalities when put behind the wheel of a vehicle. Once they get on the road, people who in the workplace have a relaxed attitude to time suddenly seem to be in an awful hurry. In addition, for some reason a significant number of them seem to prefer driving in the extreme inside lane on the wrong side of divided highways to driving on the legal side (which in Thailand is the left). When we first saw a motorbike with pillion passenger steaming along at high speed down the wrong side of the highway we wondered if we should report the incident to the police. We lost interest in the idea when we realised the two carefree spirits on the bike were dressed in police uniforms!

Measured by the death rate per 100,000km of travel, Thailand is rated the sixth most dangerous country in which to drive after Namibia, Swaziland, Malawi, Iraq and Iran (www.worldlifeexpectancy.com/cause-of-death/road-traffic-accidents/by-country). A high proportion of the casualties are bike riders.

Small-business risks

Another risk faced by the foreign small-business entrepreneur is getting ripped off by a Thai partner. Elderly men who enter business partnerships with young Thai brides met in a bar someplace are particularly susceptible to this fate. It is entirely possible that the young female from an impoverished up-country family sees her wealthy foreign male companion more as a business opportunity than as a loving partner. When all the money that can be extracted has been extracted, the young bride may decamp.

Stories of disappointed foreigners whose Thai partners took advantage of them are a dime a dozen. One hardworking acquaintance of ours invested his savings in a hardware supply company only to come to store one Monday to find the premises stripped of stock, fittings, money and Thai partner. Another foreigner who brought a lawsuit against a Thai customer for payment of a debt was visited by associates of the delinquent creditor, one of whom placed two bullets on his desk then promised to visit again to deliver the bullets at higher velocity if the lawsuit wasn't dropped.

In less extreme circumstances courts will schedule mediation between the contesting parties. If mediation fails, the case goes to court, where it may take to two years to be heard. Stories abound of disputes between foreigners and Thais that courts resolve in favour of Thais. An unknown number of foreigners in Thailand, mostly older men, who have lost their money in unsuccessful business ventures, but lack the funds for an air fare to return to their countries, are trapped in Thailand as poverty-stricken illegal immigrants. Some of the lessons to be learned from stories of failed joint ventures in Thailand are the same as they could be anywhere:

- Go into business for business rather than personal reasons.
- Be cautious with business partners.
- Try to learn what is motivating your Thai partner before entering a business arrangement.
- Tread carefully when extending credit to customers.

Skills development

Part of the government's grand plan to turn Thailand into the next Asian Tiger is to develop a skilled workforce. The Department of Skill Development (DSD), operating under the Ministry of Labour, exists to further this aim. The act which the DSD administers is the Skill Development Promotion Act B.E. 2545. Under this act, employers in specified areas with at least 100 employees are obliged to contribute to a labour-training fund at a rate not higher than 1% of the wages bill. In return companies, are granted:

- Tax deduction of 200% of the cost of training their workers either as pre-employment training or skills upgrading
- Exemption from VAT for equipment used for training
- Deductions of charges for utilities at twice the cost of training expenses

Unskilled labour

On visiting Thailand, foreigners from the West may be struck by the preponderance of individuals performing menial tasks. There seems to be an awful lot of people whose role in life is to open and close gates, direct traffic, attend doors and work as security guards. These people are almost invariably obliging and friendly, assisting staff members, and quite often complete strangers, move bags and enter and leave car parks.

But you might find yourself wondering in this age of automatic door openers, CCTV and motion detectors, are the jobs these people perform really necessary? Our conclusion is probably not. But for a reasonably sized enterprise, these people are expected, and apart from their standard duties of opening gates and assisting you park your car, having employees stationed outside the premises does provide an added layer of security.

Any significant commercial operation will come equipped with an attended security gate operated by a human being rather than a card reader. For gated communities the security guard may, as a token of security, ask visitors to deposit some document, such as a driving licence or a passport, at the gate. Many of these gates are manned 24 hours a day on a two-shift basis. Anyone costing a project in Thailand should consider including a significant security detail operating at somewhere near the minimum rate of pay.

Establishing contacts with customers

In most aspects of business, Thais tend to work through networks to a greater degree than Westerners. This may pose problems for foreigner entrepreneurs entering the country who haven't got a network to start with. Of course an implied condition of contract when going into business as a joint venture is that Thai partners will supply contacts through their own networks. But in addition to this, foreign entrepreneurs will benefit by developing networks of their own.

Since Thais value face-to-face contact to a greater extent than Westerners, your prospective distributors/partners will expect you to visit Thailand before entering into a contract with you. Setting up meetings with prospective partners should pose no problems since business contact with foreigners is particularly valued within Thailand.

Thai businesses tend to be hierarchical with less interaction between levels of the organization chart than in the West. When introducing yourself to a potential customer for the first time, try to make contact with the most senior person available, preferably the CEO. Mid-level managers in Thai companies are a great deal less likely to take initiatives than in the West and a great deal more likely to be in awe of their bosses. If you are fobbed off to a mid-level manager, whatever the strength of your message, the chances are that it won't get passed up the chain of command.

That said, getting access to the boss can be much easier for a Westerner than for a Thai. By and large Thais still tend to believe that Westerners in specialist occupations are gifted with special talents they lack. They generally welcome foreigners, their ideas, their investments and their products.

Chapter 8

Getting the Best out of your Stakeholders

Office culture

A popular view is that Thais working at middle-management level and below carry into their offices attitudes stemming from their rural backgrounds. Activities such as sowing and harvesting are controlled by external forces, such as weather, that move capriciously, at their own pace and direction, well beyond human influence. Like farmers waiting for the monsoon to break, Thais are seen as patient people. For many of their transactions they need to be. Government agencies and the bureaucracy, in particular, take their time. Thais are accustomed to forming slow-moving, orderly queues at places like post offices and banks.

As stated previously, other influences reinforce this culture of resigned acceptance. Buddhism shares with many religions the view that setbacks of the present, if accepted graciously, will be compensated by rewards in a future life. Childhood conditioning at home and at school reinforces the belief that an individual's place in the hierarchy of life has been preordained and is unchangeable.

For the younger generation, this early conditioning may be modified by the homogenising influences of movies, mobile phones, internet contact with the outside world, and by university culture for those who go on to attend a tertiary institution.

But Thais with less educational advantage seem to bring much of the culture of religion, home and school to the workplace. In this view, Thais in middle management and below tend to be reactive rather than proactive. Their patience, while commendable, is at odds with the modern-day commercial world's frantic pace of meeting ambitious schedules and beating impossible deadlines. Middle-management Thais have a reputation as eager order-takers but poor delegators who allow uncompleted tasks to accumulate in their in-trays rather than either completing them or passing them on to others to do.

Thai office culture tends to be evolutionary, not revolutionary. Thais in middle management may let things happen as distinct from making them happen. Thai bosses play their own part in cementing these attitudes. They micromanage their staff to a much greater degree than is customary in the West. They tell subordinates how to perform their tasks, rather than defining the task and allowing subordinates to go their own way. Poorly conceived orders are likely to be meekly obeyed without question. Poorly defined tasks languish untouched in in-trays.

To circumvent these cultural roadblocks, some Western employers in Thailand prefer employing Thai graduates straight out of university rather than employing older people entrenched in cultural attitudes of a bygone era. Others quit using Thais for middle--management tasks and instead employ foreign managers more attuned to their own culture. Still others accept the status quo and find ways to work with the Thai staff provided by their Thai partners.

Hierarchies

Western society appears flatter than Thailand's ordered class structure, where family connections and length of service rather than ability determine promotions. The passive attitudes of Thais in middle-management positions and the autocratic style of their bosses may rankle foreign managers more accustomed to meritocracy.

For those not born or brought up in Thailand, social status inside the kingdom is a little more ambivalent. For years Thailand has been a favoured stamping ground for people from the West on vacation, and more recently from other parts of Asia, most notably Japan and China.

As well as vacationers, a significant population of foreigners come to Thailand on other missions. Some arrive as business people, foreign managers or entrepreneurs. These individuals tend to be from the higher social strata of their own countries. They bring with them money and a sense of privilege. In most cases they are afforded even more privilege when they arrive in Thailand as heads of their organisations or suppliers of specialist expertise.

Another category of foreigner spending time in Thailand is the Western retiree, to whom the primary attraction is Thailand's low cost of living compared to home. Retirees from Europe, who might struggle financially in their home country, can live a reasonably high-status lifestyle in Thailand, perhaps with a servant or two, financed by pensions paid by their home country governments. In the Thai view these visitors are categorised by the single faintly derogatory designation "*farang*" – a word that is thought to have its origins in the word "France", from a couple of centuries ago when French colonial ambitions in the region were at their zenith.

Just how the average farang is regarded by Thais is somewhat indeterminate, perhaps for no better reason than farangs themselves are a broad spectrum of sex tourists, budget retirees stretching their dollars, wealthy retirees who have migrated to Thailand as a second home to escape the Northern Hemisphere winter, wealthy entrepreneurs, and well-connected business people. On the surface, Thais of all social classes are generally polite and obliging to their foreign visitors. But since the majority of farangs don't learn Thai beyond a very basic level, a common local assumption amongst Thais is that a farang within earshot will be unable to understand a Thai conversation.

If you want to know what Thais really think of you, learn the language!

Being the boss in Thailand

Foreign managers need to expend a higher level of effort in Thailand developing workplace relationships than in their home offices.

Fostering a caring culture in the workplace becomes a significant part of the working day, but pays dividends. Managers in Thailand take a much greater interest in the personal lives of their subordinates than in the West. Light and polite banter is expected in most circumstances before introducing the subject of work into a conversation. This patronage shows that the caring foreign manager acts like a Thai manager would in discharging a supporting role for his staff.

As in any managerial role dealing with staff, good practice is to learn people's names as early as you can. This may pose special problems in Thailand as Thai names tend to be incredibly long, and therefore difficult to pronounce, let alone remember. Fortunately Thais have invented their own solution to this difficulty by the widespread use of nicknames – mostly mercifully short. Thus, Suvannaporn might be known as Daeng, and Bunchanachai might be known as Mai. People acquire nicknames that other cultures might think are derogatory, for example Moo (pig) and Lek (shorty). Around a Thai office it is entirely appropriate, in fact normal practice, for the boss to address people by their nicknames, perhaps respectfully prefaced by the second-person singular pronoun, *khun*.

Bosses are also expected to create social occasions now and again to entertain their staff. Whatever bills that arise from such events should be picked up by the boss without question. Gifts to staff to mark special occasions are also widely acceptable, even expected. As an employer, you should never be seen to be mean in granting small favours. Any generosity extended to your staff, both of spirit and in the material sense, will be rewarded later one way or another.

Frankness versus Kreng jai

As an expat manager in Thailand, one of your major problems will be extracting information from your staff – particularly concerning problems and setbacks your business may be experiencing. In the expat's office back home, getting the facts and dealing with them directly, openly and honestly is the normal way of working. Frankness is valued. People are advised to speak their minds clearly and plainly.

Less so in Thailand.

In the Thai language there is a phrase that is hard to translate and explain, because in the Western world the concept doesn't exist. The phrase, *Kreng jai,* describes the way Thais keep relationships pleasant and co-operative and accounts for much of the politeness and civility of Thai society. *Kreng jai* underlies your Thai staff's aversion to asking questions in meetings or their reluctance to disturb you with an important telephone message when you seem otherwise occupied. If you are a boss who is intense and driven, *kreng jai* may well be the standard response from your staff as they sit dumbstruck in meetings while you are calling the shots.

Given that ineffective communication is thought to be one of the reasons that organisations run into problems, many management books stress the importance of transparent, clear communication. Despite the textbook model, in the real world clear and transparent communication often runs up against that overwhelming force – cultural conditioning. For a variety of reasons, human beings in organisations may like to keep secrets from each other. Typical motives are competition amongst employees for promotion and other advantages, and various versions of the well-documented human tendency to "kill the messenger". Bearers of bad news rarely fare well in any society, and Thailand, where bad news is barely considered polite, is no exception. It is much easier, at the moment of telling, to share with our bosses the news they would like to hear, even if doing so creates bigger problems later.

If Thais have some bad news to impart, they generally won't lie about it, but likely won't volunteer it. If the bad news is a delay, Thais are more likely to withhold information while figuring out ways to make up lost time. On the well-accepted principle that authority can be delegated, but not responsibility, Thai staff may consider that since management makes all the decisions, it should know all aspects of the business. Thai staff may feel that management, and not they themselves, are responsible for whatever goes wrong. Foreigners running projects in Thailand need to spend plenty of time and effort updating their schedules, uncovering the reasons for delays, and working around them.

Should you, the manager, try to create a more Western-style environment, where employees are empowered to take initiatives? This is a moot point really, with arguments for and against.

Changing Thai attitudes would be against deep-seated local cultural norms as would changing Western attitudes in a Western business environment. Thai staff may lack ambition and enterprise by Western standards, but generally they are hardworking and conscientious to a fault. By exhibiting *kreng jai,* Thais are trying to be polite to you and honouring your position as boss.

Over time, continued efforts to show that you are patient and receptive to employee's questions, opinions and objections may lower the *kreng jai* barrier to allow the passage of useful, if less than welcome, information.

Staff meetings

Formal assemblies of staff under Thai management tend to be structured affairs. Thais send out invitations to meetings far and wide. This tends to turn meetings into speeches from the boss to the assembled masses.

Out of the office, Thais tend to talk all the time. But at a staff meeting, conscious of their level in the hierarchy, staff members are more likely to sit, listen and take notes on matters that concern them. Brainstorming is not typically an agenda item at a Thai staff meeting. Staff may be reluctant to suggest ideas and likely to endorse whatever they think the boss wants to do, whether they agree with it or not. Raising questions might imply that information from the chairperson was inadequate or incomplete.

Meetings held in English compound the problems for Thai attendees. By the time a Thai staff member has figured out what was said, mentally translated it mentally into Thai, thought out their response in Thai and translated it back into English, the meeting might have moved on to its next item. Meetings held in Thai are more likely to have the staff contributing ideas, but will require the presence of a translator to assist a foreign boss not fluent in Thai.

Agendas are unfortunately rarely circulated prior to the

meeting. Circulating an agenda would increase the chances that attendees figure out in advance not only their position on an issue, but also how they can express it. As a further measure to encourage contributors, you can check people's ideas prior to the meeting, discuss and agree what your Thai attendees will say, and at the meeting compliment them for saying it.

Handling criticism

An important matter in the Thai notion of hierarchy is the issue of "face". As a general rule, no one should be taken to task in front of his or her peer group. Embarrassing employees in front of their colleagues is gravely offensive, more so than in the West.

But eventually there may come a time when you have to point out to someone that he/she is doing something wrong. In the West an employee is usually disciplined as soon as the mistake is discovered. But given the face issue, a better strategy in Thailand is to wait for a suitable moment when you can see the erring staff member privately, then keep things pleasant by balancing criticism with praise. By contrast, praise should be given in public – it will raise the face of the meritorious staff member.

Keeping cool

A force that drives relationships inside and outside the workplace is the Buddhist "middle path" of peace and harmony. The person who is, or appears to be, serenely indifferent (*jai yen*) is respected for possessing what is considered a virtue. Around the office you will frequently hear the phrase *Mai pen rai,* which translates roughly to "Don't worry about it" or "It doesn't matter", in relation to something unfortunate or unplanned that has occurred. While this philosophy tempers feelings of conflict and anxiety in the present, and enables calm acceptance of mishaps and mistakes, it is less likely to find a solution to the problem.

Westerners may appreciate and value relationships with their Thai co-workers and generally welcome a warm working environment. By being results-oriented, those who never have time to smile or say hello to their Thai staff risk being labelled as too serious. Management systems that have been tried and tested at headquarters back home may not necessarily fit the Thai model.

Planning the office layout

Thais have a different notion of personal space from Westerners. Thais like to socialise, interact with one another and, above all, have fun wherever possible. The word for work in Thai is *ngan,* which is also the word used to prefix a celebration, a festivity or a social function. To a Thai, labour, temple, fair, birthday party and employment may all be seen in terms of social gatherings, encapsulated in the word *ngan.* This does not mean that Thais cannot distinguish between work and play. It simply reflects the fact that a Thai's private life and professional life meld together. Thais see their work roles as relationship-oriented rather than task-oriented. They don't make clear distinctions between social relationships and work relationships. Friendships easily cross the line between work and social life. For this reason, Thais are less likely to feel they are in competition with other staff members than their counterparts in Western companies, and more likely to see themselves as team players.

One consequence of this is that instead of aspiring to their own office, Thai staff may be content to work in a communal bull pen cheek by jowl with their friends. On the other hand, as in the West, a personal office recognises seniority and status. When planning the office layout, an expat manager is advised to give thought to balancing these competing preferences in the minds of staff members.

Working inside the box

One of the characteristics engendered by both the Thai sense of preordainment and an educational culture that discourages open-minded enquiry, is a tendency to work within narrow limits. Office workers have their own job. They might be prepared to work for hours without complaint on the most tedious of tasks, but suggestions that they might expand their portfolio of talents to meet some new job requirement will likely not be greeted with enthusiasm. They may have already decided they are sales clerks/ photocopy machine operators/chauffeurs since that's what you hired them to do. They are comfortable in their jobs. They may not want to switch roles to other jobs, or even (in your eyes) to better jobs. One of the downsides of this thinking is that if someone goes missing, no one will want to take on the missing employee's job, even on a temporary basis.

Timeliness

Thais aren't quite as ruled by the clock as are Westerners. Meeting deadlines is less important. Projects tend to run behind schedule until near the end. Then when all looks lost, projects get completed on time in a flurry of last-minute activity.

As one expat said about Thailand, "In the US we are practically at the point of ulcers in order to keep our time schedules. Here in Thailand I learned that sometimes the best thing to do is to relax about some things, and they'll take care of themselves."

Thais also tend to have a relaxed attitude to appointments. Thais quite often cancel appointments and meetings at short notice when other things crop up demanding their attention. This is one area where those working in Thailand might be advised to diverge from local practice. If timekeeping and schedules are important to your operation, you have the opportunity to set the example to your staff by your punctuality and adherence to schedules.

If your meetings are in Bangkok, traffic jams – whether real or imaginary – are the standard excuse of participants who show up late. Traffic jams in Bangkok are so normal that you are unlikely to get a phone message from your missing callers who are running behind schedule. Common practice is to assume that the missing personnel are stuck in traffic someplace – or will later claim they have been.

For those inclined to operate to critical-path schedules, this casual attitude to time can be a source of irritation. For example, you would be unwise to assume that if some delivery programme is not running to plan, the Thai staff-member responsible for the programme will keep you informed. Progress in completing urgent tasks should be closely watched.

Dressing up and dressing down

Outward appearance matters in Thailand. Your standard of dress is a symbol of rank. From makeshift shelters, broken-down shacks and public areas under bridges, Thais can emerge immaculately clad and perfectly groomed. Since many Thais with minuscule resources manage to achieve miraculous results in the dress and hygiene area, if you are a farang manager you are advised to at least match the grooming standards of your business associates.

In business settings, tattoos and nose and mouth piercings are not highly regarded, although earrings are acceptable. Though religious tattoos to ward off evil spirits are becoming more visible as dress codes are relaxed, and tattooed girls are also evident in greater numbers than the past, at time of writing Thais likely to be of most value to most business activities are generally those occupying the lower end the body-decoration spectrum.

On the subject of dress, while the dress code for your company will depend on its own culture, those visiting Thailand on business are well advised to go formal than casual. Barring information to the contrary, businessmen should wear a tie and at least carry a jacket. A business suit is appropriate dress for the business woman. In a work environment, as elsewhere, feet are not a highly regarded part of the human anatomy. Shoes for men are mandatory; shoes for women preferred, though sandals are now becoming acceptable business footwear for women (though it is still preferable to keep the heels covered).

When one of the foreign embassies in Bangkok held a National Day celebration a few years back, the ambassador decided to project a friendly image and dress down for event. This move was not a success, merely serving to embarrass the well-dressed Thais of high social rank who attended the evening event.

Message: if in doubt, err on the side of dressing up, not down.

Managing your partner

As has been previously mentioned, of all the stakeholders having an influence on your business prospects, your Thai partner might well be the most relevant to the success or otherwise of the enterprise. It is worth bearing in mind that your Thai partner will have been exposed to the same cultural influences as your staff. This might, for instance, manifest itself as a reluctance to pass on bad news for fear of jeopardising the harmony of the partnership.

Working for the boss in Thailand

If your role in the organisation is working for a Thai boss rather than being the boss yourself, you are not expected to overdo "going Thai" to accommodate the cultural norms of your host society. Within reasonable bounds, you can afford to be more assertive and opinionated than the typical Thai employee, and take more liberties than Thais of equivalent rank. As an expatriate employee, your employer and your colleagues in the organisation are likely to assume that you have superior knowledge and expertise in your area of operation. Within limits you can also impress your Thai colleagues and betters with your versatility. Foreigners may be admired for their wider-ranging skills (should they happen to have any) but should avoid straying too far outside their major discipline.

In addition, a certain status flows to your boss from having you around. You may find yourself taken to meetings with important people discussing subjects that seem to bear little relevance to your role in the organisation. After a few such meetings you may realise that you are filling a mascot role. From the point of view of your Thai boss, having a foreign expert on the payroll is seen as a token of success for his organisation. Your boss may be showing you off to stakeholders not for your consummate skills but to raise his own image and prestige within his peer group.

Results versus Relationships

While to an extent Thais will expect their expat bosses to keep their distance in line with their higher status, they are more likely to respond to a manager who is friendly, visible, and shows that he or she is trying to look after their interests. But how do you manage to maintain a balance between getting the job done without putting pressure on staff relationships?

Here are a few suggestions:

- Ask yourself, "Do I really know my Thai staff?" Do you know where your secretary's hometown is and what your sales manager's favourite sport is? With Thais you do need to let them know that you care about them, though without going so far as counselling them about their private lives.
- Don't do anything that distances yourself from your Thai employees. For example, when Thais buy snacks to eat in the office, they always buy a little extra so there is enough to share with the other employees. This explains why you find plates of fried banana or some other snack placed near the coffee urn in the office kitchen. Distributing snacks and treats to your staff now and again shows that you are one of the team, not merely head of the team.
- Offer your staff shared incentives aimed at creating and maintaining a consistent and happy team rather than emphasising individual competition and individual rewards. That said, a letter to a Thai staff member signed by the director to recognise an accomplishment will be appreciated and costs nothing.
- Request deadlines rather than order them. Your statement that "100 widgets must be produced in 12 months" might be changed to a request of "How many widgets do you expect to produce in 12 months?" This puts less pressure on the relationship between you and the staff and allows staff to participate in goal-setting.
- Thai staff tend to develop loyalty to a person rather than to an organisation. It is common to hear of popular department managers quitting an organisation and his whole work team following her or him. This exodus might have no relation to salaries and benefits offered by the company. Before

you remove a department head, consider who else you will lose if he or she goes.

- Helping others in the office accumulates goodwill and obligates recipients of your goodwill to help you at a later date.
- The importance of relationships should be extended to your customers as well. Invite your top customer to inspect your factory and follow the inspection with a dinner or lunch invitation.

The hierarchy gap

As a final word in this section, it might be noted that while Thai bosses are portrayed as terribly empathetic to their staff, this is motivated by the self-interest of creating a productive office that benefits the business bottom-line. Our experience is that this solicitude doesn't extend to highly dispensable employees at the bottom of the organisation – gate-keepers and the like – who from one day to the next may barely be acknowledged as the boss's Mercedes sweeps majestically into its front office parking spot. By and large high-ranking Thai's connect very sparingly with members of the lower orders with whom they may have the occasional fleeting contact. Their concern is for more intermediate members of staff with whom they are more intimate and who are of more use to them.

Staff social activities

Managers will benefit from providing opportunities for social encounters among the staff. For example, a card and a cake is usually purchased for a birthday. A staff outing or two during the work year is normal for Thai firms. Alternatively the staff may take the initiative. There will be the times when you are invited to a family function such as a wedding or to a New Year Party. On such occasions certain protocols apply.

Weddings

If you receive an invitation to the wedding of a staff member, it is up to you whether you attend or not. It's not exactly rude to turn the invitation down, but the attendance of an expat manager at the wedding of a staff member is perceived by some hosts as a source of pride. So unless more pressing matters require your attention, it probably pays dividends in goodwill if you accept the invitation. More likely than not you will find the wedding is set for a weekday since the date is chosen by a Buddhist monk based on auspicious astrology rather than your work programme. In this case, since most of your staff will also be invited, rescheduling of office work may be required.

A Thai wedding consists of two ceremonies. It begins in the morning with a blessing ceremony, during which monks bless the bride and groom and the wedding guests as well. Guests typically sit on the floor while monks chant blessings. After the ceremony, the monks will then be offered food. If you are required to make a food offering to a monk, the same rules apply for serving food to monks as have already been described for the blessing of company premises. In the afternoon, the water-pouring ceremony (*rot nam sang*) takes place, where guests gather to pour holy water over the couple's hands. A dinner reception ends the day, and you may have your photo taken with the bride and groom and may be asked to give a speech (which you should keep very short – particularly if delivered in English).

Whether you attend the wedding or not, you are advised to provide a gift of money. Your contribution should reflect your seniority within the company. A staff member will be able to suggest an appropriate amount. Money helps in covering the dowry or "bride price" and expenses of the wedding. Your gift should be placed in an envelope marked with your name and company and given to the bride and groom or taken by yourself, or someone else, to the reception desk at the entrance of the function room if that is where the wedding is taking place. You will receive in return a little souvenir prepared by the couple. The fact that you receive no further expressions of gratitude does not mean that your contribution has gone unnoticed or is unappreciated. The wedding couple did not accept the gift personally and it is most unusual for Thais to send written notes of thanks.

Funerals

Thai funerals may stretch over a number of days and nights of chanting and other ceremonies by monks – the duration of the funeral relating to the status held by the deceased in his or her community. The body of the deceased will remain in a casket for however many days are deemed appropriate. People of immense importance have been held in this state over a year before being cremated.

If one of your staff members dies while in your employment, the employing company is expected to host at least one of the evening ceremonies, sponsor the monks and donate to the temple. This is particularly the case for a close personal friend in the company or a low-status employee, such a gate attendant, whose family might struggle to meet the funeral costs. An additional cash contribution to the deceased's family will also be appreciated. In Thailand, giving money is not seen so much as a gift but rather as making merit or *tham bun*. Ask a Thai colleague to suggest an amount appropriate for a donor of your status. If you and the deceased were not close, or if you decide not to go to the funeral for some reason, have an office colleague take your *tham bun* money along with them in an envelope to present on your behalf.

At the temple, the casket is placed on a stand and decorated with fresh flowers and wreaths. A portrait of the deceased will rest against the coffin or be placed nearby. To honour the deceased, the company should arrange a floral wreath bearing your name or the name of your company.

Funerals typically start with an evening of chanting by monks. Sometime during the evening, drinks, finger food and sweets may be served. Similar ceremonies will be held the following days. At the end of the mourning period, the body is cremated at the temple. The cremation service runs for about an hour and a half. Guests are expected to place a small decorative item, such as a flower made from wood shavings, on the casket immediately before it enters the furnace. As each guest exits from the crematorium they are given a souvenir such as a keychain, book, or other small token as a reminder of the deceased person.

In contrast to the West, the traditional colour for funerals in Thailand is white, though with Western influence black is becoming more commonly worn. Women typically can wear either colour but probably not both. An expat boss attending a company-sponsored funeral will typically wear a dark suit and tie.

One hundred days after cremation, another ceremony is held at a temple (not necessarily the same temple as the funeral) to pay respects to the deceased. Attendance by the expat boss at this ceremony would be appreciated, but is not generally expected.

New Year parties

There are three New Years in Thailand:
- The Gregorian New Year is 1 January.
- Chinese New Year, determined by the lunar calendar, typically falls in late January or early February.
- Thai New Year (Songkran) is in mid-April.

Gregorian New Year

For the Gregorian New Year, your office will most likely work a half-day, after which an extended lunch should be provided by the company with games, music and an exchange of gifts between staff. Days beforehand, expect that socially inclined staff members will be busy making arrangements for the event. Alternatively the half day off and games may occur on New Year's Eve with New Year's Day a full-day holiday. At a minimum an expat boss is expected to give presents to direct subordinates. The value of the gift is determined by the relative roles and status of the giver and the recipient as well as the nature of the relationship. Keep the gifts simple so as not to embarrass the recipients. New Year's may be an appropriate time to reward staff performances and to offer gifts to customers and those who have been helpful to your business.

Chinese New Year

Chinese New Year is celebrated by street parades that feature an impressive cast of dragons and dragon-dancers. Red and yellow lanterns and bunting are hung from convenient fixing points in public spaces. An official one day's statutory holiday is awarded to recognise the event.

Thai New Year

The traditional Thai New Year's Day (Songkran), between 13 and 15 April, had its origins as a gentle water festival to celebrate the coming monsoon. Some would argue that the present version of this idea has got out of hand with people in pickup trucks roaming the highways and byways seeking targets to hose down with water from high-pressure pumps. Others regard the day as a lot of fun. Three days' holiday is granted for Songkran. Companies don't need to make any special provisions for this day other than give their employees a day off work.

Status symbols

Thais are as much into status symbols as anyone else. To indicate their status they use the same expensive toys – gold jewellery, flashy cars, fancy apartments and so forth.

Apart from money, titles are also handy. Thai business men who have retired from the defence forces (Thai businessmen fairly typically have a military or police background) retain their titles for use in public circles. In addition to their full-time business positions, Thais may hold high-status positions as professors at leading universities even though they haven't taught there for years and these roles barely pay an income. Mobile people don't lose status as they move from one role to another, but collect their titles and honours along the way.

As anywhere else in the world, Thais use business cards on which they might try to up their status a little. A card that shows the position Head of Cash Receipts Department rather than Assistant Accountant might elicit more respect from the card's recipient.

Other Thai values

The Thai language has a number of words and phrases for feelings and emotions which don't translate exactly into English but which shape Thai relationships.

Hai kiat
The act of *hai khiad* means to show someone respect or honour. When a boss attends the wedding or funeral ceremony of an employee, takes the time to greet his staff by name and stop to chat, or asks advice from his employees, he is expressing *hai khiad* to his staff. This creates feelings of indebtedness in the employee that will one day be returned.

Nam jai
In Thai, *jai* means "heart", a word that is associated with other words to express feeling (or lack of it), along the lines of "cold-hearted" and "warm-hearted". Putting the two words *nam* and *jai* together gives "water from the heart", which has a meaning something similar to the English saying, "the milk of human kindness". *Nam jai* means to extend kindness to others without the expectation of anything in return. For example, a stranger on the street has extended you *nam jai* if you find yourself penniless and they give you money for the bus ride home.

Hen jai
To *hen jai* or to "see heart" means the ability to understand or empathise with people. When you give someone the day off to look after a sick relative you are displaying *hen jai*.

Sam ruam
Sam ruam stems from the concept of the "middle path". Thais exercise restraint in situations which, in the West, might trigger strong emotions such as anger, frustration, or sadness.

Gender bias
Clear-cut separation between males and females is learnt from a young age. In adolescence, girls are shielded by their parents and taught to avoid sex until after marriage while boys are more or less left to do whatever they like. Thais seem to accept male infidelity as normal. Keeping a major and a minor wife (*meea noi*) was widely practised in the past and is not uncommon today.

The Thai view of sex can seem a double standard to foreigners. If you are a man, you may be invited by a male colleague to go *thiaw phuying* (visiting a massage parlour). However, around the office if you do so much as give your secretary a friendly pat on the back for a job well done, for the rest of your stay in Thailand you may acquire a reputation for groping the female staff.

An NGO consultative group reporting in 2001 found that 53% of the Thai workforce were women. High concentrations of workplace females were found in the garment industry (90%) and in manufacturing (67%). Multinational garment companies set up to take advantage of cheap labour rates employed mainly women as manual workers, and men in supervisory roles. Women are also prominent in agriculture and amongst street vendors and elsewhere in the informal economy. On average the consultative group found that female workers in manufacturing were paid 30% less than men.

In 2000, Thailand passed legislation prohibiting discrimination against women in the workplace. But as in most countries, this legislation is difficult to enforce. In many occupations, seniority in the workplace is men's prerogative. Much of the glass ceiling in Thailand is still pretty well intact.

In 2003, the Thai parliament had 12 female members (9% of the total seats, against an average for democracies around the world about double that). But as a sign of changing times, in 2011 Thailand had its first female PM. And in 2012 Thai Airways International raised the retirement age of its female flight attendants from 45 to 60 – to match that of males doing the same job. Thai women now hold top jobs in occupations like teaching and media.

Nevertheless, Thailand is nowhere as sensitive to sexist language as the West. Job ads may be worded along the lines of "Manager wanted, 30 to 35 years of age, Thai national, *male only*". Or *"Pretty Thai girls between 20–25 for receptionist position"*.

Checklist – Do's and Don'ts

Without excessively generalising, Thai employees readily develop a sense of teamwork. They support their employers and their fellow employees. They easily accept orders. On the flip side, compared to Western cultures, Thai employees may seem to lack spontaneity and individuality.

Here is a summary of Do's and Don'ts around the workplace:

Do:

- Make your employees feel valued. Take time out to find out about their lives and interests outside the working environment. Try to engage closer members of your staff in small talk occasionally.
- Remember that Thais enjoy a great sense of ceremony. You will be well thought of if you mark the birthdays of your closest staff with a small gift.
- Share things around, such as food brought into the workplace.
- Try to ascertain what resources staff might need to get their work done more efficiently. Staff may be reluctant to point such things out to you.
- Entertain staff as a group now and again. Taking staff out for an outing, at your expense, is expected and enhances relationships.

Don't:

- Don't assume, unless you have good reason to do so, that directions you have issued have been understood. Thais are more likely to guess what they are meant to be doing than ask questions that would make them absolutely sure.
- Don't be reticent about displaying your skills.
- Don't criticise members of your staff in front of their colleagues.
- Above all, don't lose your cool. Loss of temper, indicating loss of control, is the surest way to lose face in Thailand.

Chapter 9

Communication

The Thai language

The Thai language is thought to have evolved as a discrete language about 2,000 years ago, its origins probably lying in the more ancient Chinese languages of the region, with significant influences from Pali and Sanskrit. Until the second half of the 13th century, Thai was a spoken language only. The first known written text in Thai dates from 1292AD. King Ramkamhaeng, on the throne at that time, is considered by some to have created the Thai alphabet. Linguists in Asian languages regard this claim of royal lineage as an oversimplification, possibly even a myth. But it remains a popular view in a society that is inclined to confer on royalty credit for projects as varied as seeding clouds, aerating fish ponds and predicting the future.

The Thai alphabet has 46 consonants (of which two are obsolete); vowels and vowel clusters (combinations of more than a single vowel) number 36. Vowel sounds can be long (as the *a* in "bath") or short (as the *a* in "cat"). As in English, in some cases the same vowel sounds can be made from different combinations of vowels clusters. However, unlike English, each written vowel or vowel cluster can only pronounced in one way, with the result that pronunciation of vowels from written texts is regular.

That's the easy part.

The most difficult aspect that Thai presents to the English-speaking learner of Thai is the five tones – mid, low, falling, high and rising. Unless you use at least three of the tones correctly, many Thais may not understand what you are saying. In fact they may not realise you are trying to speak Thai! The two tones you could consider merging while you master the basics of the language are the low tone, which is almost indistinguishable from the mid tone (i.e. no tone), and the high tone, which is similar to the rising tone. That will leave you with a more manageable and distinctive set of three tones, mid, rising and falling. This is enough to get you by.

Tone rules are complicated. Firstly there are three classes of consonants (high, mid and low), two classes of vowels (short and long) and three classes of syllables (stop, sonorant and medial) that together determine the tone of each syllable, for a total of 18 possibilities. In addition, syllables may or may not get a "tone marker" shown above the vowel. Where a tone marker occurs, its tone will override the regular rules of pronunciation. There are therefore a total of 24 possibilities for correctly determining the tone of each syllable.

In written Thai, many of the vowel sounds are *implied*, which is to say *omitted* from the written word. You see a written word with two adjacent consonants crying out for separation by a vowel, but which vowel do you choose? There's no telling. You either use your best guess, or you know because you have learned the word before.

Further complications ensue with consonants. To learners of Thai, consonants seem to be far more numerous than they ought to be, since their number exceeds by no small margin the number of consonant sounds the language contains (similar to "c" and "k" in English, but far more numerous). This is OK for reading, but difficult for correctly writing the spoken word (which of the range of consonants available do you use for a particular sound?). As a result, spelling of pretty much every word in Thai has to be memorised. Add to that the rule that most consonants make a different sound at the end of syllable and at the beginning of a syllable, and that a single consonant can sometimes be used to make both of these two sounds, you start to wonder what King Ramkam-haeng might have had on his mind when he invented the written language. For instance, there are six different letters at beginning of a syllable and 15 different letters at the end of the syllable that make the "t" sound.

One theory is the king was influenced by his monks, who wanted to complicate written Thai so that reading and writing would remain beyond the pernicious influence of peasants toiling in the fields. If so, the monks were successful – at least for a while. As with most languages, the written word was initially restricted to centres of learning, which at that time were Buddhist temples.

On the other hand, the Thai language has simple grammar rules. Object follows subject. There are no genders, plurals, articles, almost no tenses and few prepositions. Vocabulary is formed by combinations of simpler words – a little like German. For example the word for "sock" is a combination of the word for "foot" *thao* and the word for "bag" *thung*. Thus a sock is *thung thao* – a "foot bag" (like French, in Thai the adjective goes after the noun). Likewise, since the word for "hand' in Thai is *mue*, a glove becomes *thung mue* – "hand bag" (not to be confused with the accessory that in English goes under the same name). The word *samlor* – the three-wheeled mini-taxis very popular in Thailand – is made up of the word *sam* for "three" and *lor* for "wheel". There are thousands of other examples of combinations of small words making big words. English does the same with words like "waterfall" and "weekend", but not to the same extent as Thai.

As if all the above wasn't enough for the long-suffering farang language student, day-to-day written Thai uses a very large number of different fonts, some of which bear only a passing resemblance to the classical fonts of curls, scrolls and loops you will encounter at your local Thai language school. The fonts in newspapers and signage in streets around Thailand are so abbreviated that beginners in the Thai language may struggle to decipher the letters, let alone the words and syllables. Mass-circulation Thai newspapers, written in modern fonts that are a shorthand version of the real thing, look, to the untrained eye, like a Thai version of Wingdings.

English speakers struggling to learn Thai will be comforted to know that linguists judge Thai as a difficult language. Ratings agency Effective Language Learning puts languages into five categories of difficulty for English speakers to acquire (www.effectivelanguagelearning.com/language-guide/language-difficulty). European languages rate Categories 1–3 (easiest to moderate), while at the other end of the scale, Category 5 (hardest) includes Arabic, Chinese, Korean and Japanese. Thai is rated as Category 4.

An issue that might affect the choice of your business name is that Thai has a restricted number of sounds for ending a syllable or a word. Thais cannot end a word or syllable in the following sounds: "s", "sh", "l" and "ch". When speaking English Thais tend to pronounce "house" as "how", fish as "fitch" and "Nepal" as "Nepan". In addition, English uses a number of consonant clusters that Thai can't manage. For instance the Thai word for "stamp" (as in postage) has been taken from the English and is converted to *satam*, with the "p" omitted since the consonant cluster "mp" has no equivalent in Thai. Also note that while Thais have equivalent letters for "r" and "l" in their alphabet, in Thai the two sounds are fairly interchangeable.

Thus, when naming your business you are best advised to choose a name that can be pronounced the same way in Thai as in English. We suggest trying out your business name with a Thai speaker before lodging your incorporation documents.

Should English speakers learn Thai?

Foreign organisations working in Thailand must inevitably work in a second language to one of the parties to the transaction, or sometimes a mixture of languages. As a foreign visitor to Thailand the question is: should I learn Thai?

If you are anticipating a long-term stay, it is generally better to learn some basic phrases – correctly pronounced – from a language school, rather than try to learn a lengthy list of words from a Thai language handbook. Alternatively you can buy a speaking book equipped with CDs and learn at home or in your hotel at your own pace.

Another way to learn (after your vocabulary has reached a reasonable level) is with a non-English speaker. However, now that everyone's second language has spread so widely, non-English speakers are increasingly thin on the ground, at least in cities! Conversing with English-speaking Thais, you may find that after a few stock introductory phrases like *Sawat di khrap* ("Hello") and *Sabai di mai* ("How are you?"), Thai conversation may falter due to your limited vocabulary and your interlocutor reverts to English.

A viable alternative to learning Thai is a phone app that serves as an English-Thai translator and speaker. You enter a phrase in your home language and the phone translates the phrase into Thai and speaks it aloud. The application, Talking Thai-English-Thai Dictionary, is downloadable at a cost of about $20.

If your pronunciation is bad, Thais may be too *kreng jai* (polite) to tell you. In fact if you can manage about 50 words in Thai they will probably tell you that you *"put keng"* (speak well). Of course they're only kidding and you know it. But at least you are speaking Thai well enough for your companion to recognise that the language in which you are trying to communicate is Thai, not Mongolian!

Though Thai is the preferred spoken language, English is very much the second language. A lot of the signage in Thailand is in English, either as the principal language or as an alternative language. English is taught in primary and secondary schools, mostly by Thai teachers, generally from written texts. For tertiary education many of the textbooks and computer programs are in English while the instruction may be in Thai, or some combination of Thai and English. Overall, foreign employers are likely to find most of their staff have acquired English to some level and that the English reading skills of Thai employees are superior to their English speaking skills.

Business worldwide is increasingly conducted in English, even if neither of the parties speaks English as a first language. Thailand is no exception. More and more English-language documentation is becoming the language of commerce within Thailand – even between Thais themselves.

Oral communication

The rigid hierarchical structure of Thai organisations, combined with Thai cultural respect for authority, can increase the difficulties of oral communication in a Thai/foreign company where spoken English is the principal means of communication. For example, if your Thai employee does not understand your oral instruction, he/she is unlikely to press for clarification. Such an enquiry might involve loss of face for both parties. It might suggest the employer has failed to communicate clearly, or that the employee has insufficient skill to understand what to others might be a perfectly clear instruction.

One of the challenges Thais face in understanding oral English is its wide range of accents. Because it dominates TV and other forms of communication, American English is probably the most widely heard English accent in Thailand. But in a world where Scots and Australians may struggle to understand each other's English accents, what hope for the Thais?

So what can a foreigner do to help their Thai staff members cope with not only written English, but also the many oral versions of the English language?

If you are attempting to speak English to a Thai and are not understood, the first point to remember is to speak slowly. If that doesn't work, try simplifying your sentence by reducing the message to the present tense. For Thais, understanding tenses other than the present tense, particularly for irregular verbs, is the hardest part of learning a European language. For example Thais may not recognise the connection between different tenses such as "went" and "go", and "was" and "is". And who could blame them when according to rules of regular English (such as they are) the past tense of *go* and *is* should be *goed* and *ised*?

In the West if someone fails to understand something we say we tend to raise our voices. In Thailand this is a no-no. Thais associate raised voices with conflict. In summary, some golden rules of oral communication in a second language, or even a first language, bear repeating:

- Speak slowly
- Use short sentences
- Use present tense
- Avoid idioms and figures of speech

Even so, despite having spoken slowly and clearly in idiom-free short sentences as per the suggestions above, it is still possible you have not been understood, even though you might be unaware of it. Your Thai staff may habitually answer "yes" to any question whether or not they understand it. This tendency is magnified the higher the manager's position in the company and the greater the amount of *kreng jai* involved.

So what indicators are there that "yes" really means, "I understand" rather than "I hear you (but maybe don't understand)"?

If, having posed a question, the answer "yes" is delivered almost grudgingly, or perhaps without the expected enthusiasm, one suggestion is to watch for body language clues – a nervous stance, a worried look and a hesitant answer. Otherwise you can try open-ended questions, where it is impossible to give a *yes* or *no* answer, along the lines of "How much photocopy paper is left?" rather than "Is there any photocopy paper left?" If that doesn't work, to check comprehension you could always ask for your instructions to be repeated, although doing so might suggest you lack confidence in your staff. If you find it necessary to repeat instructions, emphasise to the listener that you distrust your own ability to give instructions, not that you doubt your employee's ability to understand.

Over time oral miscommunication will most likely occur less frequently as your staff become accustomed to your version of the spoken tongue.

Written communication

The virtues of written versus oral communication is a subject widely discussed in management textbooks by first-world authors. Oral communication is thought to be warm, personal and spontaneous. Written communication is considered more precise. When working amongst themselves in their own language, Thais are predisposed to oral communication. Rarely is a written agenda prepared for meetings between Thais. Just as rarely are minutes taken. Though Thais are inclined to oral communication among themselves, as a foreign employer, you don't need to feel too hidebound by Thai culture. No one will be offended if you, as resident foreigner, increase the output of the written word.

Comparing their relative skills of reading, writing, listening to and speaking English, Thais are most adept at reading, since the printed word is the primary resource for English teaching in secondary schools. For businesses in Thailand where the working language is English, Thais may better understand written communications than oral communications. Besides, if you provide written directives that are not understood, your Thai employee can take away your written material to a private place and mull over it with the aid of a dictionary. Or your employee can obtain an interpretation from a colleague or, if all else fails, may even approach you for an interpretation. For oral communication, he/she probably wouldn't.

Thais are less skilled at writing English than reading it. An English text directly translated from a piece of Thai writing is likely to be written in the present tense, and lack articles and prepositions, but, for all these grammatical imperfections, still be understandable to English speakers. Going the other way, from English into Thai, is equally difficult for Thai readers, particularly since Thai is a highly idiomatic language, much more so than English. Besides, Thais, being highly face-conscious creatures, may be reluctant to write in English because they fear they may embarrass themselves by expressing themselves poorly.

Another suggestion to minimise the likelihood of a round of clarifications of words written in a second language is to suggest the recipient that he can answer your correspondence in Thai or in English, whichever he prefers. In his book *Thais Mean Business*, Robert Cooper points out that for cases where you are translating correspondence that was originally conducted in Thai (say from a Thai government agency), a good idea is to attach the original Thai correspondence with the English version headed "Translation". It pays to keep both Thai and English versions on file to resolve possible translation errors.

Language of politeness

If French is considered the language of love and Italian the language of fine music, then perhaps Thai is the language of politeness. Thai has dozens of words that show respect for the differences in age and hierarchy between two people. For example, while the pronouns "I" and "you" can be used by just about everyone in the egalitarian English language, in Thai these pronouns change depending on whether you are speaking to a close friend, your spouse, a 5-year-old child, a teacher, your aunt or your parents. On top of that, if you are talking about royalty, Buddhist monks or the Lord Buddha, you would use two special, exalted forms of Thai, one reserved for royalty and the other for religion.

Languages that do not have pronouns that recognise respect for differences in age and hierarchy can be a real problem for Thais. For example, when Thais are forced to converse in English they may be denied the ability to show the appropriate respect for one another. In an English conversation with foreigners Thais will often slip into their own language to avoid using the egalitarian word "you" to another Thai whose status is either senior or junior to his own. To avoid impoliteness, Thais will refer to themselves or others by role – teacher, doctor, professor.

Apart from using pronouns to show respect, the Thai language has words that are added to the end of a sentence but have no real meaning except to show that you are trying to be polite. Males add the word *khrap* at the end of their sentences; females add *kha*. For example, if you are a man, you would say *"Sawat di khrap"* ("Hello").

Additionally, when a Thai is responding to an instruction, he or she will usually use the word *khrap/kha* to convey "I acknowledge that you have said something". *Khrap/kha* doesn't actually mean "Yes, I understand" unless it is said with the right intensity. That "Yes" and "I hear you" are communicated by the same word in Thai may sometimes be the reason why Thais appear to say "yes" to something they don't understand.

Though Thai politeness is near legendary, foreigners sometimes find themselves subject to interrogation that in their own cultures would be considered intrusive. The following queries are not unusual:

- "Hi John, I see that you are looking very fat today. What do you weigh?"
- "I heard that you have a new job in an American company. Foreign companies pay quite well. How much is your salary?"

Foreigners may feel that the bluntness of these enquiries seem out of character with the Thai philosophy of *kreng jai*. One explanation for probing into your personal affairs is that Thais are trying to determine your niche in society. Others speculate that such questions stem from the community spirit of Thailand's traditional rural roots. In this interpretation, a farmer surviving at the mercy of the elements might be unwise to assume that his neighbours were living well and enjoying adequate food and good health. In those circumstances, pointing out that your neighbour is fat or thin might be an indirect way of asking whether he has enough to eat. Asking about his salary might be a way of enquiring if he has enough money to get by. But while modern-day Thais feel comfortable posing such questions to foreigners, they are unlikely to do so between themselves where the status of contemporaries is more determinable.

The directness of these enquiries is consistent with the Thai vision of personal space. Privacy is valued far less highly in Thailand than in the West. Isolation is unusual. People expect to be with other people most of the time. Families stay together through three or four generations. Familiarity with the details of another person's life is par for the course. These attitudes are brought to the workplace. Office chit chat amongst staff is likely to be about one's personal life and feelings rather than the impersonal topics discussed in the West such as weather, sports and politics. So bear in mind that Thais mean no offence by their pointed enquiries about your bank account and dietary habits. If you find the questions discomfiting, just nod your head and smile. When Thais show interest in your income and general well-being they are just being sociable.

Telling the time

We remarked in a previous section that Thai timekeeping is not all that it could be. A possible alternative explanation, other than Bangkok traffic jams and a generally slack attitude to timeliness, may lie in the Thai clock and the Thai calendar.

Specifying the time of day is a mite more complicated in Thailand than most places. Terminology for telling the time comes from an era when the hour of the day was indicated by ringing bells and beating drums in the local temple. The terminology has persisted to this day.

For the purpose of telling the time in Thailand, the day is divided into the following segments:

- Early morning (*ti*)   1 am – 5:59 am
- Late morning (*chao*)   6 am – 11:59 am
- Midday (*thiang*)   12 pm – 12:59 pm
- Early afternoon (*bai*)   1 pm – 3:59 pm
- Late afternoon (*yen*)   4 pm – 6:59 pm
- Evening (*thum*)   7 pm – 11:59 pm
- Midnight (*thiang khuen*)   12 am – 12:59 am

To tell the time in this system, in the early morning you first specify the period of the day and then the hour. For example, 3am is *ti sam* (literally, "early-morning three"), 4am is *ti si* ("early-morning four"), etc.

So far so good – until you reach 6am.

At this point, the time format changes: now you specify the hour first, then add the word *mong* ("hour") and then the period of the day. Hence, 6am is *hok mong chao* (literally, "six hour, late morning"), 7am is *jet mong chao* ("seven hour, late morning"), and so on. To confuse matters, 7am can also be considered the first hour of late morning and thus called *nueng mong chao* ("one hour, late morning"). By this token, 8am is both the eighth hour *and* the second hour of late morning. So it goes for 9am, 10am and 11am.

Midday is midday *(thiang)*.

Early afternoon takes a new format: first you declare the period of the day, then add the hour, then the word *mong*. So 1pm is *bai nueng mong* (literally, "early-afternoon one hour"), 3pm is *bai sam mong* ("early-afternoon three hour"), etc.

At 4pm, early afternoon may or may not turn into late afternoon depending on who you are talking to. 4pm is either *bai si mong* (four in the early afternoon), or *si mong yen* (four in the late afternoon). 5pm is categorically late afternoon, hence *ha mong yen* (literally, "five hour, late afternoon"), and 6pm is *hok mong yen* ("six hour, late afternoon").

At 7pm we reach the first hour of evening, *nueng thum* (literally, "one, evening"). This period continues until 11pm, which is *ha thum* (five o'clock of the evening). Midnight can either be *hok thum* (six o'clock of the evening, or more likely, *thiang khuen* (midnight).

In all cases, minutes *(na thee)* are indicated much the same way as English, by number after the hour. Hence, 5:30pm is *hah mong yen sam sip na thee* ("five hour late-afternoon and thirty minutes").

With all that to think about to tell the time, is it any surprise that appointments in Thailand are often missed?

So if you are arranging to meet your driver at 4am to catch an early overseas flight, make sure he knows you mean the fourth hour of *early* morning, and not the fourth hour of *late* morning (i.e. 10am). One way to avoid misunderstanding would be to point to the desired hour on a clock face.

In addition, there is a simpler way to tell the time, though it is not as widely used in speech as the traditional method. Official timekeeping in Thailand is by the 24-hour clock – you'll see it printed on your airline ticket, as well as on things like bus and train schedules. By this method, 04:00 is simply *si nalika* (literally, "four o'clock"); 10:00 is *sip nalika* ("ten o'clock"); 16:00 is *sip hok nalika* ("sixteen o'clock"); and midnight – which is thought of as 24:00 rather than 00:00 – is *yi sip si nalika* ("twenty-four o'clock").

A final point of possible confusion in timekeeping is that the Thai calendar follows the Buddhist year, which is 543 years ahead of the Gregorian calendar. Though both the Thai and Gregorian calendars used the 365-day solar year plus adjustments for leap years, until 1941 the Thai lunar year started on Thai New Year's Day, sometime in April, in the Gregorian calendar. From 1941 (Thai year 2484) Thai years were rationalised to start on 1 January to match the Gregorian calendar. The 12 months of the year are the same in both calendars, as are the number of days in each the month and seven days in each week.

Thais usually express years in terms of the Buddhist calendar. If you wish to avoid confusion between the two calendars you can use the present as a reference point and express the future as "10 years' time" and the past as "5 years ago" rather than specifying Gregorian calendar years. This will allow your conversation partners to make a mental reference to their own calendars rather than having to translate from one calendar to another.

Names, titles and introductions

Thais have a first name and a surname as in the West, but no middle name. The use of the first name and family names is usually reserved for formal matters so in the office you would only come across your staff's formal names on their payslips or any outgoing correspondence they write on behalf of the company. Nearly all Thais have nicknames used amongst family and friends and in an office environment where staff feel at ease with one another.

When you are introduced to someone for the first time, the atmosphere is more formal. Here first names are used, regardless of the status of who you are meeting. Nicknames are not used by staff when addressing high-ranking people. If you are a manager of the business, it's OK for you to address your staff members by their nicknames, while they address you in return in more respectful terms.

To convey politeness, the Thai language has a variety of honorifics to use before a person's name. The non-gender-specific word *Khun* is the most common. *Khun* can be used with a person's first name or nickname. It translates roughly to the English equivalents of Mr, Mrs, and Miss.

People of higher status are given more exclusive honorifics. *Nai*, only used for males, is the rough equivalent of "Mr" or "sir". *Nai* would be used instead of *Khun* to precede a man's formal first name, rather than a nickname. Though an expat manager might rate a *Nai* if he were sufficiently important, the word doesn't "blend well" with Western names, so he'll likely be called *Khun* plus his first name – e.g. Khun David. The female equivalents of *Nai* are *Nang* ("Mrs") and *Nang Sao* ("Miss").

Than is an honorific used for males and females of high rank, such as important government servants and dignitaries – though not visiting expats. VIPs connected with royal blood, the civil service and the military have particular titles used in place of *Khun*, *Nai* or *Than* when talking in the second or third person.

In his book *Thais Mean Business*, Robert Cooper outlines royal and civil service titles. Cooper explains that royal titles last only to the fifth generation, then are no longer used. Any title should be displayed in abbreviated form on letters and invitations and the title holder would most likely use it on his or her business card. These titles appear in descending order of status as follows:

- P.O.C. – Phra Ong Chao, grandchild of king
- M.C. – Mom Chao, child of P.O.C
- M.R. – Mom Ratchawong, child of M.C.
- M.L. – Mom Luang, child or wife of M.R.; wife of M.C.

As for the civil service, in descending order they are Chao Phra Ya, Phra Ya, Phra, Luang, Khun (not the same word as the regular *Khun*), Phan/Muen, and Nai.

If Thais hold, or have held, important positions such as university lecturers, then they may use the word *A-charn*, meaning "teacher", in front of their first name even if they have retired. Similar rules apply for military personnel.

Titles that you may encounter that apply specifically to women are *Khunying* and the higher title of *Thanphuying*. Each year the king bestows these titles on women who have "contributed to the development of the country or whose support has been crucial to the success of their husbands". These titles are used in place of *Khun* or *Than* before the first name. You will often see the names and faces of various *Khunying* and *Thanphuying* in the "high society" pages of the Thai daily newspapers.

Hierarchy of the body

The parts of one's body are part of a hierarchy – in relation to other body parts and to the external environment. The head is seen as the seat of one's "soul", and is treated with the greatest respect. With some exceptions, touching the head of another person is taboo. In addition, many Thais spend a great deal of time grooming their hair and that of their children, and don't appreciate having their crowning glories disturbed. Of course medical and dental treatments are exceptions to the rules on body contact. Head touching within family and between those in intimate relationships is also in order. Touching the heads of small children is generally acceptable for family members and close friends, but not for strangers.

Body hierarchy applies not only to your interaction with people, but in some cases to your interaction with objects. For example, many Thais wear Buddhist amulets or a miniature picture of a royal member on a necklace. If a Thai offers you such a gift to be worn later, once you've finished admiring it and conveyed your thanks, put it in your highest pocket, such as your top shirt pocket not in a trouser pocket or a skirt pocket close to less respected body parts. Alternatively you can place the object in a bag.

In the hierarchy of body parts, on the opposite end of the scale from the head, physically and socially, are the feet. Thais share with many other cultures the belief that the feet are the lowliest and dirtiest part of the body. Your feet are there purely for functional reasons such as walking, driving cars, playing sports and riding bikes. Don't use your feet for purposes such as indicating to your mechanic which of the tyres on your car is flat or, to a staff member, the location of photocopy paper on the lowest shelf in the stock room. Placing your feet on the desk is a definite no-no. Nor should feet be used to open doors. While it is generally acceptable to sit cross-legged at a table or a desk, honorary guests sitting high on a stage in front of an audience are advised to keep their feet grounded if they can.

Shoes, by extension, carry the feet's lowly status. A foreign manager once shocked the Thai staff at an exhibition in Bangkok when she used her shoe as a hammer to affix a Thai flag to her exhibit!

Hand gestures

When talking, avoid the hand-waving habits commonly associated with Italians and Greeks and those with a nervous disposition. Thais converse with a minimum of physical gestures.

Putting your arm around someone or slapping them on the back for a job well done is not a habit of Thai people. Finger-pointing at objects is acceptable, but not at people. If you have to distinguish someone in a group, the polite way to do so is to point with palm facing upwards and fingers brought together.

If you need to pass something to someone, Thais don't like you to throw it no matter how small or insignificant the object. The traditional way to pass business cards, books, sheets of paper and the like is with both hands. When passing an object to a superior with one hand, Thais will most likely use the use their left hand to support the right hand holding the object.

Touching

Because of taboos on touching someone of the opposite gender, the safest greeting between men and women meeting for the first time is to say hello with a polite smile, and a nod of the head. Shaking hands is best confined to those who understand the gesture. Thais who have had little contact with the outside world are confused as to who offers their hand first and how many shakes to make, so are unlikely to initiate a handshake. Thais who have lived in the West, on the other hand, are quite used to the practice. Feel comfortable to shake hands with Thais who offer their hand, regardless of gender.

As for more general contact, touching someone of the opposite sex in public is considered inappropriate unless you know them well. If you are a male and you feel one of your female staff has done a great job, don't express this by patting her on the back. Thais can read unintended meanings into such things. An exception to this rule is attracting the attention of a female friend or colleague by tapping her on the elbow. Touching someone of the same sex is fine. Don't be surprised if colleagues of the same sex take your hand while talking to you. Keep the contact going until they release you.

Wai-ing

The *wai* is the ubiquitous Thai greeting that has no real equivalent in the West – a way of saying hello and goodbye, conveying thanks, showing respect to others, and acknowledging sacred objects such as Buddhist statues and spirit houses.

It is performed by raising both hands, palms together, fingers held up upwards. Elbows are kept close to the body as the hands are raised. The position of the hands in relation to the head is all-important. A junior will wai with hands at the top of his head which is bowed forward slightly. When two Thais meet, the junior person in age or social rank wais first. The senior may wai in return with hands a little above chest level, or may merely nod his head or smile to acknowledge the greeting. The greater the difference in status between two people, the less likely the superior will return the wai. At the top of the social hierarchy, Buddhist monks never return a wai from anyone, not even the king or queen, who, in turn, never wai to the public. There is no gender difference in waiing: the same rules apply to males and females.

As an expat you will receive plenty of wais in Thailand. The question is, should you return them? Or, if you are really bold, initiate them? As a guideline don't return a wai from those a great deal lower than you in the social hierarchy – even if the young child waiing is very cute, or if you think the guard who wais you at the gate when you arrive at the factory deserves one in return. To return such a wai confuses people, and makes you look silly.

Just acknowledge any wai you receive from a social inferior with a smile and a nod of the head.

Office staff will generally wai you when receiving their pay, when entering or leaving your office or when delivering a message to you when you have guests. A smile and a nod are sufficient to acknowledge these gestures.

The safest people and objects to wai are monks, Buddha images, and elders other than servants and street vendors. It's always safe to wai your important business or government contacts when you greet them and take leave. We are also advised that a policeman or a government bureaucrat who has helped you in some way will appreciate a wai, if properly executed.

If someone wais you when you have your hands full with a mobile phone or briefcase, don't feel it necessary to put everything down before returning the wai – just lift your hands into the closest wai position you can manage without dropping anything. Otherwise, if you are holding a newspaper, for example, tuck the newspaper under your arm then wai.

The finer points of waiing take time to master. For example, to wai with a pair of shoes in your hands is impolite since shoes are associated with feet, the lowest of the low in terms of body hierarchy. This happened to a foreigner who had taken off his shoes before entering a colleague's home. When his colleague's mother emerged from a room to greet him, shoes in hand he gave what he thought was a deeply respectful wai. The shoes turned a well-meaning gesture into a gross insult.

If you think you've mastered the art of waiing but are with a group of foreigners who don't know how to wai, it may be better to offer a handshake or nod, to prevent your foreign friends feeling awkward. If they see you wai they might think it necessary to wai as well, initiating a domino chain of clumsy waiing that could be embarrassing all round.

The smile

Thailand has acquired a justly earned reputation as "The Land of Smiles". Except at immigration desks at the airport (for which a stern demeanour seems to have been prescribed), Thais smile at great deal.

As we have already described, Thais do have a great sense of fun *(sanuk)*. Also they make light of situations that citizens of less fun-loving nations might be inclined to take seriously. In fact, Thais are so serious about displaying the light side of life that their language contains a veritable sub-vocabulary of terms categorising smiles by type. In their book *Working with the Thais*, Henry Holmes and Suchanda Tangtongtavy list several varieties:

- *Yim thang nam taa:* The "I'm so happy I'm crying" smile
- *Yim thak thaai:* The polite smile for someone you barely know
- *Fuen Yim:* The stiff smile, also known as the "I should laugh at the joke though it's not very funny" smile
- *Yim mee lessanai:* The smile which masks something wicked on your mind
- *Yim haeng:* The dry smile, also known as the "I know I owe you the money but I don't have it" smile
- *Yim chuea chuan:* The "I am the winner" given to a losing competitor.

If the authors of *Working with the Thais* are right, this list goes some way in explaining why Thais smile so much. They smile when they are happy, admiring, amused, unamused, sad, wistful, disagreeable, victorious, brave or dismissive – a list that leaves little not to smile about. Whatever the motivation, to the recipient the smile is disarming, and whatever else happens, smiles in the Land of Smiles help make the Thailand experience enjoyable for its visitors.

Entertaining

Entertaining business colleagues, customers and staff is pursued with enthusiasm in Thailand, in line with the more general pleasures of widening social contacts and enjoying life. The following is a list of suggested Do's and Don'ts relating to entertainment and the wider social environment.

Smoking

Tobacco smoking is not as prevalent in Thailand as it is in places like Germany, Russia and China. In many areas, such as enclosed public buildings, public transport systems and airports (with the exception of dedicated rooms for smokers), smoking is prohibited. It is probably accurate to say only a small percentage of Thais smoke in the workplace. If you are a smoker, whether you should smoke in your office is a matter of judgement. Thais are likely to be too *kreng jai* to ask you not to smoke. If they don't smoke themselves, their general reluctance to express disapproval for social blunders you might make should be taken into consideration.

Alcohol

There are no taboos in Thailand against drinking. Many brands of beer are available, both local and imported. Beer is generally served cold and often taken with ice. Wine drinking has become more fashionable in recent years. Most wine is imported from Europe, South Africa, the Americas and Australasia. Local winemaking is now an embryo industry, with at least four vineyards having been established in Thailand in the past 20 years.

The spirit of choice for men is whisky, of which local and imported brands are available. Local and imported whiskies are only vaguely similar, being the same general colour but quite different in taste. Thais are particularly brand-conscious about their whiskies. In a restaurant situation the whisky bottle is kept in a prominent position on a drinks tray beside the table, its label displayed for other patrons to admire. Whisky is usually taken with the meal rather than after. Thai whisky drinkers generally mix their tipple with soda water or (to the dismay of foreign whisky connoisseurs) with cola! Diners at Thai restaurants should note that waiters tend to hover over tables, topping up half-empty glasses on their own initiative, thereby making a mess of your alcohol consumption estimates.

Imported whisky makes a most acceptable gift for business colleagues and customers. If whisky is your gift of choice, buy an expensive brand. Johnny Walker Black Label is the minimum accepted standard. Going down-market sends an unwelcome message to the recipient of stringent budgetary limits to your largesse.

Eating out, bill paying and tipping
The principal cutlery items used by Thais are spoons and forks. Spoons are held in the right hand, forks in the left. Chopsticks are often provided as an alternative for dishes like noodles. Except in Western-style restaurants, knives are seldom used since Thais cut meat into small pieces prior to cooking and the flesh of fish can be separated with the fork.

Thais don't use their fingers except for food that can't be handled any other way such as cracking crustacean shells. They often share common dishes, and sometimes may not be too fussy about using a common spoon to convey their selections from the common dish to their plates.

After a meal it is socially acceptable to use a toothpick. Thais will sit happily around a table chatting away while picking at their teeth, concealing their activities with a hand or a serviette. Thais do have a problem with people blowing their noses around food. Spitting is not acceptable, although some of the older-generation Chinese Thais are yet to lose this habit.

In Thailand the rules of bill-paying are simple. If it's a business meal, the senior person pays unless it's pretty obvious someone else is hosting the meal. If it's a social occasion, to avoid an awkward discussion at the end of the meal make it clear before ordering that you intend to pick up the tab. Bill-splitting amongst Thais is rarely done. "American share", as Thais term this practice, suggests to Thais that everyone is stingy, including themselves!

Tipping in Thailand is not widely expected, at least from Thais, who are inclined to scrutinise every detail of the bill prior to paying, while a nervous waiter hovers close by. If you wish to tip, you might check your bill, because many upmarket restaurants and hotels follow the Western practice of adding a 10–30% service charge.

Extracurricular activities

It is well known that men in Thailand may easily avail themselves of free-and-easy relationships with the opposite sex. A constant supply of women, particularly from poor rural districts, is despatched to urban centres, often by their families, to service this market. Sex workers send as much of their earnings as they can to their impoverished families back in the village. If you're a lone male business traveller in Thailand, quite likely you will receive an invitation to a massage parlour, a brothel, or a nightclub/restaurant where sex is offered as a side dish. It is quite OK to turn down an invitation from your boss to visit a brothel or pseudo-brothel without making an excuse. If you do accept you are not obliged to avail yourself of the entire suite of services on offer if you prefer not to do so.

Chapter 10

Infrastructure and Environment

Telecommunications

Under the rules of Thailand's Foreign Business Act, foreigners are banned from participating in media in Thailand. No foreign-owned newspapers, radio stations or TV stations operate in the country.

The Telephone Organization of Thailand (TOT), which built the fixed-line telephone system, was founded by the Thai government on 24 February 1954. In 2003, during the prime ministership of Thaksin Shinawatra, an additional government organisation, the Communications Authority of Thailand (CAT), was formed to take care of international telephonic communications. At that time Thaksin had ambitions of privatising the industry. Since he was already the owner of telephone company AIS (Advanced Information Services), this led to allegations of conflict of interest.

Political in-fighting about regulating the industry continued for a number of years. Thaksin's plans to privatise the entire phone system were cancelled by the military after the coup of 2006. In December 2009, TOT became Thailand's first 3G mobile phone service provider. In 2010 the National Broadcasting and Telecommunications Commission was formed to regulate the industry and allocate frequencies among service providers.

Joint-venture businesses with 49% ownership have been allowed in telecommunications since 2006. However, all three major privately owned service providers are Thai companies. In order of size they are AIS, DTAC (Total Access Communication Public Company Limited) and True Corporation plc.

Though most of the telecommunications territory has been carved up between these three private companies (one substantially owned by a former PM), wrangling continues among the three and the regulator about who gets what. Lack of clarity from the regulator has slowed the uptake of new technology. So have recent political disturbances preventing the budgets of TOT and CAT from being approved.

At time of writing, 3G technology is widespread across Thailand and 4G technology is available in some areas. Internationally the country is connected via submarine cables to Asia, Australia, the Middle East, Europe, and US, as well as two satellite earth stations.

Phone charges in Thailand are inexpensive. More so than in most countries, people tend to buy phones outright and either prepay their calls, or buy a plan tailored to suit their particular needs separately from buying the phone. To get you started when you first arrive, a SIM card that will most likely work in your phone can be bought at the airport for about 150 baht.

Broadband internet started in Bangkok and Chiang Mai and has been expanding quickly. For fast data transmission, construction of a fibre-optic cable system is underway, with customers able to access high-speed internet, television and telephone from one fibre-optic cable network connection. As with most of the world, this industry is changing so rapidly that any statements made about it are likely to be out of date in a few months. Up-to-date information about internet and cable TV in your area of interest can be obtained from the three competing commercial companies.

There are about 30 free-to-air Thai-language TV channels in the country, with a mix of government and private ownership. A choice of plans from three different cable providers offers satellite and cable TV with a wide range of local and foreign content. In Thailand as everywhere else, cable and satellite TV make foreign influences difficult to curb.

Thailand has 480 radio stations, some private and some public. Programming is similar to Western countries – music and talk shows and lots of ads. Public broadcasting falls under the aegis of governmental Public Relations, which is responsible for Radio Thailand, the official radio station of the country. It transmits all the local and international news mandatorily broadcast by all Thai stations. Radio Thailand is also the direct channel for government information. Most of the major government ministries have dedicated radio stations. At 8am and 6pm, the national anthem is played on all stations, which at busy urban centres is broadcast over PA systems. When the national anthem is heard on PA in a public place, people pay their respects by stopping whatever they are doing and standing to attention.

Print media

Bangkok publishes two English-language daily newspapers, the *Bangkok Post* and *The Nation*, each with circulation of under 100,000. Both of these papers are Thai-owned and have a sober tone with no particular political viewpoint. The Thai-language papers cater to a greater range of tastes – from sensationalist to soberly conservative. The largest-circulation Thai newspaper is *Thai Rath*, a fairly conservative paper by Thai standards. In aggregate, Thai-language newspapers outsell English-language newspapers about ten to one. The biggest-selling Chinese newspaper is the *Sing Sian Yit Pao*.

Foreign magazines for niche markets among the foreign community in Thailand are allowed, subject to FBA ownership rules. A number of English-language magazines are published in Bangkok, with circulations of 4000–5000 copies and funded either by subscription or through advertising. English-language local newspapers in towns such as Pattaya and Hua Hin, which have substantial foreign populations, are also permitted. The content of local papers is targeted to the interests of expats rather than national and international events. Content on the local social scene – what's moving in real estate, the latest changes of immigration rules, and buying and selling of goods and services – typically dominate their pages.

Electricity

The largest electricity generator in Thailand is the mainly state-owned but partially privatised company, EGAT (Electricity Generating Authority of Thailand). EGAT delivers electricity to customers through two distribution entities. The Metropolitan Electricity Authority (MEA) is the distributor for Bangkok, while the Provincial Electricity Authority (PEA) distributes power to the rest of the country. Consumption is split 46% industry, 22% domestic, with the balance for commercial use.

Thailand is a net importer of electrical power. Electricity comes over the southern border from Malaysia and from hydro generators in Laos to the east. Electricity produced within Thailand is predominantly generated from natural gas (71%) followed by coal 21% and hydro 5%. At present only 2% of the country's electricity is from non-hydro renewable energy, most of that from biomass.

This energy mix is of some concern to Thai authorities conscious that the life of the known gas fields in the Gulf of Thailand is about ten years. Currently the preferred fuel for the future is imported coal but this is less than ideal since not only does imported coal add to the nation's import bill, but it is environmentally damaging.

Renewable energy projects and energy saving projects, both on BOI's list of desired industries, represent opportunities for foreign investors.

Domestic power in Thailand is 220V AC at 50Hz. Three-phase power at 415V is supplied for industrial users if needed. Plugs on domestic devices and 240V connections have improved over the years, though not to the extent of being completely reliable. Power outlets still come in a range of styles, two flat or round pins and in recent years, two flat or round pins with an earth pin. In previous years plugs were notorious for falling out. Most current plugs don't fall out of sockets quite as easily, but some do. Those equipped with earths are not only safer but also more inclined to stay in place. For US and Japanese imported devices working at 100–120V, transformers are widely available, as are adaptors to enable unlike plugs and sockets to be connected.

The reliability of power supply has improved in recent years as Thailand strives to improve its industrial image. Growth of electricity demand has averaged about 5% per annum since 2000. Growth of installed capacity has increased by nearly 6% per annum in the same period. According to Global Network Institute, Thailand was 98% electrified in 2005; only a few villages in the remote north lay outside the grid.

Water supply

Water is piped to about 75% of the population in Bangkok by the Metropolitan Water Supply Authority of Thailand. Much of the water for Bangkok is drawn from artesian wells since by the time the Chao Phraya River reaches Bangkok it is too polluted to serve as a water supply. In the medium-range future, falling water tables may jeopardise water supplies in Bangkok unless other sources can be found.

Outside Bangkok, water is supplied by the Provincial Water Supply Authority (PWA). Overall PWA serves the domestic demand of about 60% of the population living within its jurisdiction. It is not unusual for homes not supplied by town water to pump their water out of wells into holding tanks at their properties.

During the first decade of the new millennium, Thai water authorities have faced an increase in industrial demand for water of about 20% per year, a demand which they have struggled to meet. Thailand still has the capacity to increase its water supply considerably from 25 major river catchment areas with rainfalls between one to two metres per year without resorting to energy-intensive measures like desalination plants. Also additional water storage capacity is being constructed as part of flood mitigation measures currently underway. According to the literature, industries setting up in BOI estates and industrial parks are assured a water supply. However, this point should be checked during due diligence before signing a contract to set up your business – particularly if your enterprise is a heavy water user that you intend to locate outside a certified industrial park.

Roads

For years Bangkok has been notorious for its traffic jams and pol-luted air. In Thai the word for traffic jam is *rot tit* – derived from the Thai words *rot* ("vehicles") and *tit* ("connected"). A couple of radio stations focus entirely on traffic information, 24 hours a day, seven days a week. Drivers call in with updates on *rot tit*, helping other drivers plot intricate pathways through the congested city. Nevertheless, despite their best endeavours, every now and again streets are blocked for hours on end. Some recount that during the height of this crisis on the roads, taxi drivers carried vessels in their cabs for use should they have needed to answer a call of nature while trapped in interminable gridlock.

While traffic jams still plague Bangkok, and radio *rot tit* contin-ues to do business, car travel in the city is quicker and easier than it was ten years ago. Over the last 15 years, improved roads and alternative transport systems and freeway extensions have eased traffic snarls.

The Skytrain, an overhead rail system (the Bangkok Mass Tran-sit System, or BTS), was opened in 1999. After initial doubts that sufficient numbers of Thais would pay the fare (an average of around 30 baht for a one-way ticket), the system has been well patronised. Trains are almost always full, carrying about 600,000 passengers a day. The BTS has been extended four times since was first opened. Further extensions are underway.

While this was going on aboveground, Bangkok also built an underground railway system. Opened in 2004, the Metropolitan Light Rail System – more widely known as the MRT – currently has 18 stations and transports 240,000 people per day. In 2011, construction was started on extensions to link the city stations on a circular track and to connect outer city areas not currently serviced.

Toll roads in and around Bangkok have also been extended and upgraded.

Apart from infrastructure growth, another thing that has helped ease congestion in Bangkok has been a successful policy of low population growth. The population of the country, 67 million at present, has nearly stabilised, thus decreasing the need for new infrastructure. All in all, traffic flow in Bangkok is a lot easier and air pollution a lot less today than it has been in the recent past.

Further afield, traffic flow around the country is generally good. Traffic in Chiang Mai, the second most populous city in Thailand, flows reasonably freely, as it does in Thailand's numerous smaller cities. Most major highways between cities are dual carriageway, of reasonable quality but generally not grade separated. They are adequate for the mixture of truck and personal traffic they carry.

In the past, Bangkok suffered a well-deserved reputation for air pollution. However air quality has improved, in particular after 2003 when the city banned two-stroke motors from its motor bikes and *tuk tuks* (small taxis converted from motorbikes). Buses with no emission controls were also removed from service.

Bangkok air remains more polluted than in comparable Western cities, but is a great deal better than cities in China, Iran, Pakistan and India. Air quality has been measured by the World Health Organisation (WHO) for various cities in parts per million (ppm) of particulate matter less than 10 microns in diameter. In 2009, against an average of 71ppm over the 1100 cities listed, Bangkok returned a measurement of 54ppm. By comparison with other cities in the region, air pollution in Singapore measured 29ppm, Kuala Lumpur measured 49ppm and Beijing (which is not the most polluted city in China) measured 121ppm.

Airports and airlines

Bangkok's first commercial airport at Don Muang reached its full capacity in the early 2000s with little possibility for expansion at the site. A new airport, Suvarnabhumi Airport, which had been discussed for many years, was started in 2002 and completed in 2006. Built to compete with Singapore and Kuala Lumpur as an Asian hub airport, Suvarnabhumi has capacity for 40 million passengers a year (compared to the present tourist numbers for 2013 of 26 million, over 80% of whom arrived by air). Suvarnabhumi has now replaced Don Muang as the main airport into Bangkok for a mix of international and domestic passenger traffic, with Don Muang primarily handling freight and domestic flights. At present the only international airline that uses Don Muang is Air Asia, which returned there from Suvarnabhumi in 2010.

Suvarnabhumi Airport is located about 25 kilometres east of Bangkok, with easy freeway connections into town, and direct access to Highway 9, Bangkok's outer ring road tollway that encircles Bangkok and discharges its traffic load to all points of the compass both into Bangkok and out to the provinces. The airport also has a rail connection to the city from a station in the terminal building at Suvarnabhumi. The trip to the centre of Bangkok takes about 30 minutes by normal train, 15 minutes by express train and maybe 30 minutes by taxi – depending on the destination in the city and the state of the traffic. Suvarnabhumi is also handy for getting to the eastern province of Chonburi, where much of the country's heavy industry is located. An expansion currently underway at Suvarnabhumi is to build an additional terminal, which will raise annual passenger capacity by a further 20 million to 60 million.

Five other locations in the country have international airports – Chiang Mai, Chiang Rai, Hat Yai, Phuket and Rayong/Pattaya (U-Tapao Airport). Another 20 destinations have domestic airports or airfields.

Rail

The State Railway of Thailand (SRT) manages the country's railways. There are five main routes, all of which originate in Bangkok. The longest goes south, down to the Malaysian border. The second longest goes north to Nong Kai, two stations north of Chang Mai. In addition there is one route to the northeast, another to the east and another to the southeastern coastal provinces. In all, the network has about 4,500 kilometres of track.

For most of these routes the rail connection is a single track, something that doesn't favour high-speed travel. According to all accounts, the SRT has been losing money for a long time. Nevertheless, despite being slow and practically always late, trains are comfortable, cheap and well patronised. According to SRT, the system carries 50 million passengers per annum. But rolling stock hasn't been upgraded for years and the track and its associated gear are poorly maintained.

New funding for rail was announced in 2012. Since moving a ton-mile of freight uses only a fraction of the energy that trucking requires for the same distance, rail freight is attractive for the energy-conscious Thai government.

A major rail project currently underway is to build a parallel track from a freight consolidation yard at Suvarnabhumi Airport to Thailand's busiest port, Laem Chabang, in Chonburi Province on the eastern seaboard of the Gulf of Thailand. This project is part of a five-year plan to expand Laem Chabang port. Rail-freighting containers will reduce road traffic, save energy and reduce atmospheric pollution from greenhouse gases – all declared government objectives under its BOI programme.

Since Thailand is located at the hub of Southeast Asia, goods travelling by surface transport from Singapore and Malaysia must go through Thailand to reach anywhere else in Asia. A much larger project that has been on and off the drawing board for about half a century is the Trans-Asian Railway project, intended to connect Kunming in southern China to Singapore. The Chinese have already started the part of the project within China. If it ever gets built, the rail connection would re-energise rail travel in Thailand and surrounding countries. While principally for freight, the line would also offer passenger services. One snag is that rail gauge for the Southeast Asian countries is one metre, whereas China's rail gauge is 1435 mm, the standard for most of the world. Laos, which doesn't have an existing railway in the required location but has narrower track elsewhere, has tentatively agreed to go with standard gauge of the Trans-Asian Railway. The Chinese plan at gauge-change locations is to piggyback smaller trains on the standard gauge bogies rather than transfer the goods from one train to another.

This project requires much cooperation between the Chinese and ASEAN nations. It has been discussed for many years, but hasn't yet got the go-ahead. But if/when it does Thailand would likely get about half their rail system upgraded, which would be of tremendous benefit to freight movements within the country.

River transport

Some of the most heavily populated and highly industrialised areas of the country are situated in Thailand's fertile drainage basin of the Chao Phraya and its two major tributaries, the Ping and the Nan. Rivers in the Chao Phraya system flow south through the central plains of Thailand from sources in hills and mountains to the north, east and west, passing a number of cities and major towns along the way before emptying into the Gulf of Thailand at Bangkok. For years Thais have used this waterway for transporting goods and raw materials to and from the capital and between cities and towns en route.

Not so long ago, in the days when Bangkok was called the "Venice of the East", canals were the principal means of bringing fresh produce to market. Now the klongs of Bangkok have largely been filled by buildings and infrastructure. The remnants of yesteryear's floating markets in Bangkok now do very little real trade other than as tourist attractions. But rivers still act as commercial waterways. Materials still travel up and down the Chao Phraya in dumb barges strung together in groups of three or four and towed by tugs. Barges each carry about 2,000 tonnes of bulk cargo such as rice, sugar, logs, sand, cement or backfill from construction projects. Cargo for export is taken to deepwater ports in the Gulf of Thailand for transfer to bulk carriers. Further information on this subject for those interested in moving bulk cargo along the rivers of Thailand can be obtained from the Port Authority of Thailand (PAT) (www.port.co.th/pat/index2-eng.html).

In addition, about 50,000 Bangkok commuters per day use Chao Phraya ferries to get to and from their workplaces, embarking and disembarking at piers between Pier 1 to the north of Bangkok and Pier 34 to the south.

To a lesser extent, cargo moves along the Mekong, where this major river defines the nation's eastern and northern boundaries.

The Mekong is a much larger river than the Chao Phraya, but has less Thai industry on or near its banks. That no Thai seaport is available at the mouth of the Mekong to ship the goods to overseas markets makes the Mekong a less attractive commercial route than bringing goods down through Bangkok.

Ports

Ports in Thailand are administered by the Port Authority of Thailand. The first port to be built in Thailand to handle large sea-going ships was Bangkok Port, completed in 1951 on the mouth of the Chao Phraya. As cargo ships increased in size, an additional deep-water seaport was needed.

At present, Thailand has the following major ports besides Bangkok:

- Laem Chabang in Chonburi Province, the first stage of which was completed in 1991, is Thailand's biggest port. It serves the nearby Industrial and Export Estates in Chonburi Province on the eastern coast of the Gulf of Thailand. Laem Chabang can handle larger ships than any other port in Thailand, but only has a depth of 14 metres. The maximum size of ships that can offload into Thailand is around 50,000 tonnes; larger ships offload in Singapore. Developments are underway to deepen wharf facilities at to 16 metres. Laem Chabang's rail extension, now under construction, will handle containers transported to a rail consolidation yard near Suvarnabhumi Airport in Bangkok. When complete, extensions at Laem Chabang will reduce importers' freight costs within Thailand as well as speed delivery of goods.

- Chiang Saen is a river port on the Mekong River in Chiang Rai Province in the very north of Thailand, nearly at the intersection point of Thailand, Myanmar and Laos.

- Ranong Port on the Andaman Sea in Ranong Province, about 600km south of Bangkok, has restricted facilities for serving

Thailand's share of the west coast of the Thai/Malaysian peninsula.

- Songkhla Port, on the southwest coast of the Gulf of Thailand, has two multipurpose ports and one container vessel facility. This port was built to promote exports from industrial estates in the region.

- Phuket Port is on the Andaman Sea and has two berths for large vessels and mooring facilities for large passenger cruise ships.

Details of the sizes of ships accommodated, the types of cargoes handled, wharf fees and other charges levied are available from the PAT website. A source of further information on Thai ports is the Bangkok Ship-Owners and Agents Association (BSAA), a membership organisation that informs interested parties about shipping into and out of Thailand (see www.thaibsaa.com/statistics.html).

Environmental legislation

The legislation covering environment is the Enhancement and Conservation Quality Act of 2535 (1992). This legislation is framed on the "polluter pays" principle. It establishes standards for industrial effluent, emissions to the atmosphere, and water quality. Under Section 46 of the act, proposed developments may be subject to environmental impact studies that must be approved by the Ministry of Science, Technology and Environment before the project gets the go-ahead.

The act also recognises third-party rights. Those who believe they are affected by development projects are entitled to query the ministry regarding the proposed development. Individuals have the right to file complaints directly against polluters and seek remedies for environmental damage caused by developments. Penalties that violators of environmental regulations face are fines paid to the government, compensation to affected third parties and possible jail sentences.

Thai culture and the commons

The view of Thais on tidiness and order are oddly conflicting. On the personal level, Thais, rich and poor alike, are scrupulous about personal cleanliness. But beyond their own skin, Thais coexist with and contribute to visual pollution which they appear to accept with indifference. Their streetscapes rapidly accumulate piles of rubbish that people step around without seeming to notice. Municipal employees might spend hours trimming a beautiful hedge at the centre strip of a roadway, while at the side of the road noodle stands sprawl across a footpath of broken slabs, and overhead a forest of loose wires dangles down from a crooked electric pole that no one thinks to straighten. Few Thais pick up litter and put it into bins. They are more likely to add to the pile.

Noise pollution is treated likewise. As a general observation, Thais consider noise to enhance most environments. Within hypermarkets piped music from three or four overlapping speakers drown out their opposite numbers in a cauldron of sound. Pickups with loudspeakers cruise slowly along streets broadcasting maximum-decibel advertising or political messages. Fixed speakers mounted on rusty poles above the foreshore of a palm-fringed beach enhance nature's picture-perfect production with heavy metal played at high volume.

Why is it so?

This mindset may have its roots in history, when property belonged to the king and the government acted on his behalf to administer the countryside. The people took no part in public affairs but waited to be told what to do by the state. Today, people still refer to public property in Thai language as royal property, highways as royal roads and public land as royal land. There is no word in Thai to match the English word "public" in its context of public land shared by the people. The word *satharana* comes close to meaning "public" but it does not reflect the concept of shared rather than individual interest. Many Thai people regard *satharana* property as belonging to no one rather than to everyone. Whatever lies outside their own property belongs to the king, who will care for it or not, according to his inclinations. Thais holding this view expect someone else to take care of the commons. But to a large extent in modern Thailand, no one does.

Future flooding?

With pressure on the environment much in the news, the view that it is someone else's problem may be changing – where there is an economic cost.

Much of Thailand's population and a great deal of its industry are located in the Chao Phraya watershed. In recent times, the infrastructure issue of most significance to both the local population and prospective investors has been Thailand's 2011 flood. Much has been written about this event and projects are underway to prevent a recurrence. The question being asked is, was the 2011 flood part of the natural cycle or was it exacerbated by climate change from human causes?

The southwest monsoon drives the rhythm of life in Southeast Asian countries from Malaysia to Vietnam. In April, as the northern hemisphere summer builds, the Asian land mass heats up, drawing moist air in from the Indian Ocean. In a normal year, the monsoon in most of Thailand (the far south is an exception) runs from May to November. For the balance of the year, prevailing northeasterly winds bring cooler dry weather.

Every year, parts of Bangkok flood to some degree during the southwest monsoon, but this usually passes without major consequence. But now and again, after heavy rain in the headwaters, Thailand experiences major flooding that severely disrupts commercial operations for hundreds of miles up the Chao Phraya and its tributaries. The central plain in which the Chao Phraya flows is very flat. For example, the town of Sing Buri, 120km north of Bangkok, is only five metres above sea level. This gradual change in elevation gives the Chao Phraya floods their curious "creeping" characteristic. Vulnerable areas downstream of flooded areas inland know weeks in advance that the floodwaters are coming. And later, what takes weeks to arrive takes weeks to drain away.

In all, 65 of Thailand's 76 provinces were affected by the 2011 floods. One of its unusual features was that the monsoon started in February, three months earlier than usual, and persisted until mid-December.

The auto industry and the computer hardware industries located in industrial estates north of Bangkok were particularly hard hit. In places floodwaters rose to three metres deep and stuck around for a long time. With their manufacturing and assembly plants out of action for three or four months until the floods abated and until damaged equipment could be restored, or in many cases replaced, some manufacturers threatened to move their plants to other countries unless the Thai government took appropriate measures to prevent future flooding. As a consequence, US$12 billion worth of flood-mitigation projects were commenced in 2012.

One obvious measure taken to reduce flooding was to help water discharge more readily to the sea by cleaning the network of canals (klongs) that pass through and around Bangkok. Another was to increase the volume of floodwaters that can be impounded and later released when rainfall abates and rainwater inflow diminishes. To this end:

- New upstream water storage areas are being constructed and existing ones modified;
- The river walls on the Chao Phraya and elsewhere are being heightened;
- Dam-management procedures have been changed to increase water release at the start of the monsoon season.

To study whether the 2011 floods were merely a blip in the long-term weather cycle rather than climate change, climate scientists scrutinised past records. Major floods in the area occurred in 1942, 1953 and 1970. Of these, 1942 was the most severe, with four times the rainfall of 2011. Photos show most of Bangkok was underwater to depths of three or four feet, suggesting that 1942 certainly matched 2011 as a major flood event, at least within Bangkok.

What's beyond doubt is that the 2011 flood caused more damage than any of its predecessors, for the simple reason there was far more infrastructure to damage, much of it belonging to companies that had set up operations in IEAT industrial parks.

The Thai government implemented its 2012 flood mitigation measures, without waiting for the scientists' decision on whether the 2011 flood was manmade or from natural causes. Reassured by the government's infrastructure activity, so far all major industries affected by the 2011 flood have stayed put.

Followers of the climate change debate currently absorbing the attention of scientists and others, tell us that different parts of the globe will be affected differently under changed climate regimes. In some areas yearly rainfall is likely to increase. In other areas it is likely to stay the same or decrease. A number of different studies for the Chao Phraya watershed have concluded that propensity to flooding will probably increase under various different climate scenarios projected by the Intergovernmental Panel for Climate Change (IPCC). If this view is accepted, government efforts to control floods along the Chao Phraya and its tributaries will need to continue into the future.

Rising seas?

A related issue of importance to Thais, in particular to inhabitants of Bangkok, is sea-level rise. Here the results are less clear-cut. Studies in the Gulf of Thailand have shown little change in sea levels in recent years, with the rise of the seabed due to geological shifts more or less cancelling out a combination of subsidence due to groundwater extraction from wells and sea-level rise from global warming. The worst predictions made at the turn of the century – that Bangkok would see serious flooding from the sea in 15 years unless a protective sea wall was built around the city – have not come to pass. But if the IPCC prediction that sea levels will keep rising globally materialise, Bangkok remains under threat. So does the hinterland, since a rise in sea level will make draining the Chao Phraya increasingly difficult.

Summary

At some point in all textbooks on corporate strategy, the reader will encounter a recommendation to those considering investing in a new enterprise to prepare a SWOT analysis listing the perceived Strengths and Weaknesses of the intended business and the Opportunities and Threats likely to be imposed by the external business environment. By way of summarising the points made in the book, we present our take on the pros and cons of establishing and running a business in Thailand:

Thailand as an Investment Destination

Strengths
- Stable industrial development plan
- Financial assistance available to investors
- Stable economy with stable currency
- Developed financial sector
- Good workplace culture
- Easy place to live
- Developed infrastructure (except rail)
- Established legal system
- Creative and imaginative labour force
- Weak trade unions
- Cheap labour
- Reasonable level of manual and management skills
- Good export markets
- Location in the hub of Southeast Asia
- Positive attitudes to foreigners

Weaknesses
- Fairly bureaucratic
- Rigorous labour laws
- Political unrest
- Moderately corrupt
- Poor rail system
- Antiquated education system
- Need to have Thai partners
- Limitations on activities in which businesses are allowed to operate
- Rules on employing unwanted labour
- Restrictions on business activities for foreign investors
- Inability to purchase land
- Highly variable English-language skills

Opportunities
- Movement of Thailand into AEC will enlarge markets
- Plans to improve infrastructure, in particular the planned Trans-Asian Railway

Threats
- Possible future flooding
- Shortage of future energy supplies
- Price rises of future energy
- Cost competition from emerging nearby economies – Vietnam, Cambodia, Myanmar and Bangladesh

Public Holidays in Thailand

Day	Holiday	Notes
1 January	New Year's Day	*Either full-day or half-day holiday*
January/ February (Lunar calendar)	Chinese New Year	*Recognition varies between provinces*
Full moon in February	Makha Bucha Day	*Buddhist day to purify one's mind*
6 April, or the following Monday if a weekend	Chakri Day	*Celebrates the founding of the present dynasty of the royal family*
13–15 April	Songkran	*Buddhist water ceremony*
1 May	Labour Day	
5 May	Coronation Day	
May (Lunar calendar)	Royal Ploughing Day	*Prediction of harvests for the coming season*
May (Lunar calendar)	Visakha Bucha Day	*Buddha's birthday (approximately)*
July (Lunar calendar)	Ashana Bucha Day	*Buddha's first sermon*
12 August, or the following Monday	Queen's Birthday	
23 October, or the following Monday	Chulalongkorn Day	*Celebrates one of Thailand's best-known kings*
5 December	King's Birthday	
10 December	Constitution Day	
31 December	New Year's Eve	

Note: Public holidays vary from region to region in Thailand. Some regions may have additional holidays. Others may exclude some of those listed above.

Abbreviations

ABL Alien Business Licence
AEC ASEAN Economic Community
AIS Advanced Information Services
APEC Asia Pacific Economic Cooperation
ASEAN Association of South East Asian Nations
BIOTEC National Centre for Genetic Engineering and Biotechnology
BOI Thai Board of Investment
BSAA Bangkok Ship-owners and Agents Association
BTS Bangkok Transit System
CAT Communications Authority of Thailand
CIT corporate income tax
CPI Corruption Perception Index
DSD Department of Skill Development
DTAC Total Access Communication Public Company Limited
EGAT Electricity Generating Authority of Thailand
EPZ Export Processing Zones
EXIM Bank Export-Import Bank Thailand
IEAT Industrial Estate Authority of Thailand
IMF International Monetary Fund
IOR Indian Ocean Rim
IPCC Intergovernmental Panel for Climate Change
ISo 9000 International standard
MEA Metropolitan Electricity Authority
MET National Metal and Material Technology Centre MET
MOSTE Ministry of Science, Technology and Environment
MRT Metropolitan Rail Transport
NANOTEC National Nanotechnology Centre
NECTEC National Electronics and Computer Technology Centre
NSTDA National Science and Technology Development Agency,
OSOS One Start One Stop
PAT Port Authority of Thailand
PEA Provincial Electricity Authority

PTT Petroleum Authority of Thailand
PWA Provincial Water Supply Authority
SBT Special Business Tax
SEC Office of the Securities and Exchange Commission
SET Securities Exchange of Thailand
SME Small medium enterprise
SPT Software Park Thailand
SRT State Railway of Thailand
SWIFT Society for Worldwide Interbank Financial Telecommunication
TAFTA Thailand Australia Free Trade Agreement of 2005
TI Transparency International
TIS Thailand Industrial Standard
TOT Telephone Organization of Thailand
TAT Tourist Authority of Thailand
TSP Thailand Science Park
TTA Thai Trade Association
VAT Value-Added Tax

Resources

Websites
Ajarn (www.ajarn.com) – Resources and jobs for English teachers
Alibaba (www.alibaba.com/countrysearch/TH/importer-list.html) – List of Thai importers
ASEAN Economic Community (www.asean.org/communities/asean-economic-community)
Bangkok Now BNOW (www.bnow.org) – Networking community
BNI Inspire (bni-inspire.com) – Networking community
Board of Investment Thailand BOI (www.boi.go.th)
Bureau of Statistics (web.nso.go.th)
Customs Department (www.customs.go.th)
Customs Valuation – World Trade Organisation (www.wto.org/english/tratop_e/cusval_e/cusval_e.htm)
Department of Business Development (www.dbd.go.th)
Department of Employment (www.doe.go.th)
Department of Foreign Trade (www.dft.go.th/Default.aspx?tabid=372) – Trade preferences and documentation
Department of Labour Protection and Welfare (www.labour.go.th/en/)
ESL Base (www.eslbase.com/schools/Thailand) – List of English schools
Export-Import Bank of Thailand EXIM (www.exim.go.th)
Food and Agricultural Import Regulations (gain.fas.usda.gov)
Food and Drug Administration (www.fda.moph.go.th)
Foreign Business Act (www.thailawforum.com/database1/foreign.html)
Foreign Business Restrictions (www.bia.co.th/005.html)
Foreign Correspondents' Club of Thailand (www.fccthai.com)
Global Market Research (www.researchonglobalmarkets.com)
Global Tenders (www.globaltenders.com/login.php)
Government Procurement (www.gprocurement.go.th)
Immigration Bureau (www.immigration.go.th)
Import Statistics (www.tradingeconomics.com/thailand/imports)
Industrial Estate Authority of Thailand IEAT (www.ieat.go.th)
International Chamber of Commerce (www.iccwbo.org)

Jobthai (www.jobthai.com) – Job listings
Ministry of Commerce (www.moc.go.th)
Ministry of Education (www.moe.go.th)
Ministry of Foreign Affairs (www.mfa.go.th)
National Science & Technology Development Agency (www.nstda.or.th)
Networking in Bangkok (www.dnndirect.com/networking-in-bangkok)
Port Authority of Thailand (www.port.co.th/pat/index2-eng.html)
Port and Shipping Statistics (www.thaibsaa.com/statistics.html)
Revenue Department (www.rd.go.th)
Siam Legal (www.siam-legal.com/Business-in-Thailand/Thai-land-Board-of-Investment.php)
Signboard Tax (www.mazars.co.th/Home/Doing-Business-in-Thailand/Tax/Signboard-Tax-in-Thailand)
Tax Booklet 2012 – PricewaterhouseCoopers (www.pwc.com/en_TH/th/tax/assets/2012/thai-tax-2012-booklet.pdf)
Thai Trade Fair (www.thaitradefair.com) – Find your trade partners
Thailand Law Forum (www.thailawforum.com) – List of lawyers
Thaitrade (www.thaitrade.com/home)
World Bank (www.worldbank.org/en/country/thailand/overview)
World Bank: Doing Business 2014 – Thailand (www.doingbusiness.org/data/exploreeconomies/thailand)

Books

BIC Publishing Co., Ltd, *Setting up in Thailand. A Guide for Investors,* 1990.

Bhikkhu, Khantipalo, *Buddhism Explained.* Silkworm Books, 1989.

Campbell, Stuart, and Chuan Shaweevongs, *The Fundamentals of the Thai Language (Fifth Edition),* Marketing Media Associates Co., Ltd, 1957.

Ch'ng, David C. L., *The Overseas Chinese Entrepreneurs in East Asia,* Committee for Economic Development of Australia, 1993.

Community Services of Bangkok, *Successful Living in Thailand,* Edited by Jennie Sharples, 1989.

Cooper, Robert, *Thais Mean Business,* Times Books International, Singapore, 1991.

Cooper, Robert and Nanthapa, *CultureShock: Thailand,* Times Books International, Singapore, 1982.

Hall, Denise, *Business Prospects in Thailand,* Prentice Hall, 1996.

Holmes, Henry and Tangtongtavy, Suchada, *Working with the Thais,* White Lotus Co., Ltd, 1996.

Moore, Christopher G., *Heart Talk,* White Lotus Co., Ltd, 1992.

Mortlock, Elizabeth, *At Home in Thailand. A Guide for Americans Living with Thai Families,* United States Information Service, Bangkok, 1986.

Naisbitt, John, *Megatrends Asia,* Nicholas Brealey Publishing, 1996.

Seagrave, Sterling, *Lords of the Rim,* Corgi Books, 1995.

Segaller, Denis, *Thai Ways,* Asia Books, 1989.

Segaller, Denis, *More Thai Ways,* Asia Books, 1989.

Segaller, Denis, *New Thoughts on Thai Ways,* Magazine Distribution Service, 1990.

Sethaputra, So, *New Model Thai-English Dictionary,* Thai Watana Panich Press Co., Ltd, 1965.

Terwiel B. J., *A Window on Thai History,* Editions Duang Kamol, Bangkok, 1989.

Toews, B. & R. McGregor, *Success Secrets to Maximise Business in Thailand,* Times Media, 2000.

Wyatt, David K., *Thailand: A Short History,* Yale University Press, 1984.

Wylie, Philip, *How to Establish a Successful Business in Thailand,* Phaiboon Publishing, 2007